Complete SUMMER SMART
Grade 2-3

Special thanks are given to
Vikalp Jain, Dev Patel, Tiffany Feler, Erica Ho, and *Marco Chang*
for their involvement in the Arts & Crafts Section.

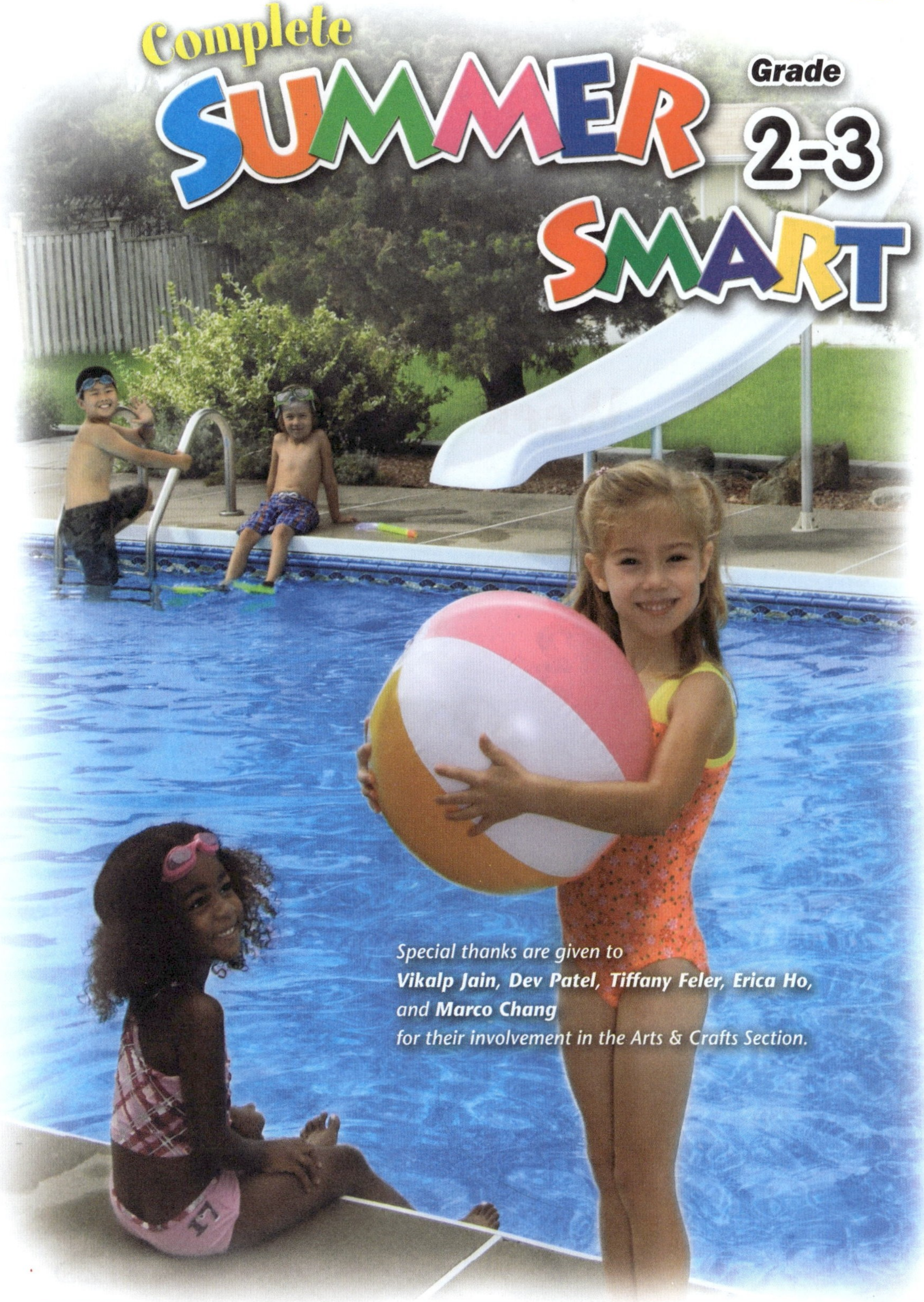

Copyright © 2011 Popular Book Company (Canada) Limited

All rights reserved. No part of this publication may be reproduced, stored in a retrieval system, or transmitted in any form or by any means, electronic, mechanical, photocopying, recording or otherwise, without the prior written permission of the Publisher, Popular Book Company (Canada) Limited.

Printed in China

ISBN: 978-1-897457-97-9

English

Mathematics

Science

Social Studies

Arts & Crafts

Contents
Grade 2-3

Week

1	5
2	25
3	45
4	65
5	85
6	105
7	125
8	145

ISBN: 978-1-897457-97-9

Safety Rules

Camping	166
Backyard Barbecuing	168
At a Beach	170
Rock Climbing	172
The Water Park	174

Answers — 177

Hands-on Activities — 191

ISBN: 978-1-897457-97-9

Dear Parents,

While all work and no play makes Jack a dull boy, all play and no work would probably make Jack forget most of what he has learned, which is why it is desirable to schedule regular practice in the long summer vacation to help your child consolidate his/her academic skills.

This is where Complete SummerSmart comes in.

Complete SummerSmart is organized in an easy-to-use format: it is made up of eight weeks (units) of work, each comprising consolidation practice in English, Math, Science, and Social Studies, followed by "Arts & Crafts" for developing your child's artistic skills. After practice, your child will be treated to some comics, and he/she will be introduced to a fun place to go in summer, too.

At the end of the book, there is a "Hands-on" section that engages your child in some fun math and language games to consolidate essential skills and concepts.

There is also an answer key for you to check the answers with your child and explain or clarify any items that your child does not understand.

By reviewing the essentials taught in the previous academic year, Complete SummerSmart prepares your child for the grade ahead with confidence.

With Complete SummerSmart, your child will enjoy a fun-filled and meaningful summer break.

Your Partner in Education,
Popular Book Co. (Canada) Ltd.

B. Colour each container to show how much of it is filled.

1. $\frac{1}{4}$ filled

2. $\frac{1}{2}$ filled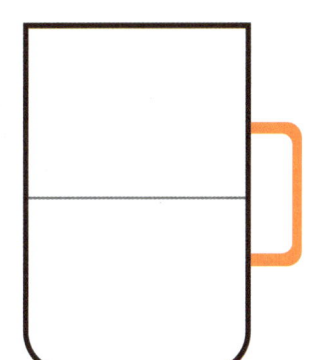

3. $\frac{1}{3}$ filled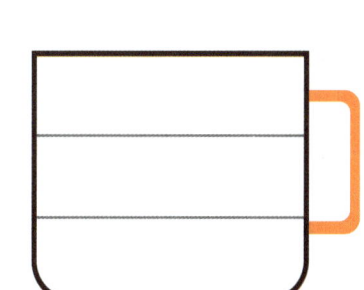

C. Look at the groups of things. Write the fractions.

1.

2.

3.

4.

D. See how much food one child eats at a party. Then draw the amount of each kind of food needed for 12 children.

1 child eats...

one sixth of a pizza | one third of a chocolate bar | one fourth of a sandwich

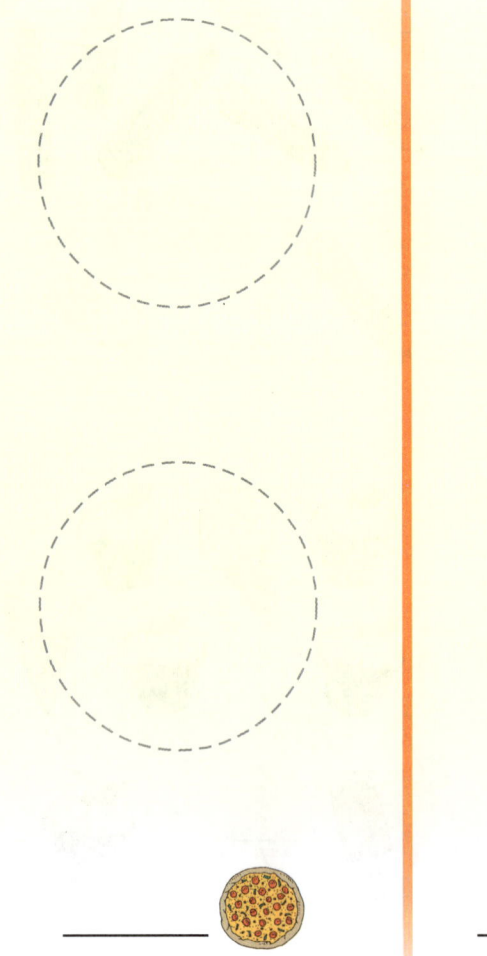

12 children eat...

Science

D. Try the experiment. Then draw to show the result and answer the questions.

1. What happened to the water level?

2. Why did it happen?

3. Where did the water go?

Experiment

a glass of water

a tape to mark the water level

Observe the glass every week for 2 weeks and record the results by marking the water level.

Result

Week 1

Week 2

97

Grade 2-3

A. Match the people with the signs.

Social Studies

B. Look at the map. Then name the places.

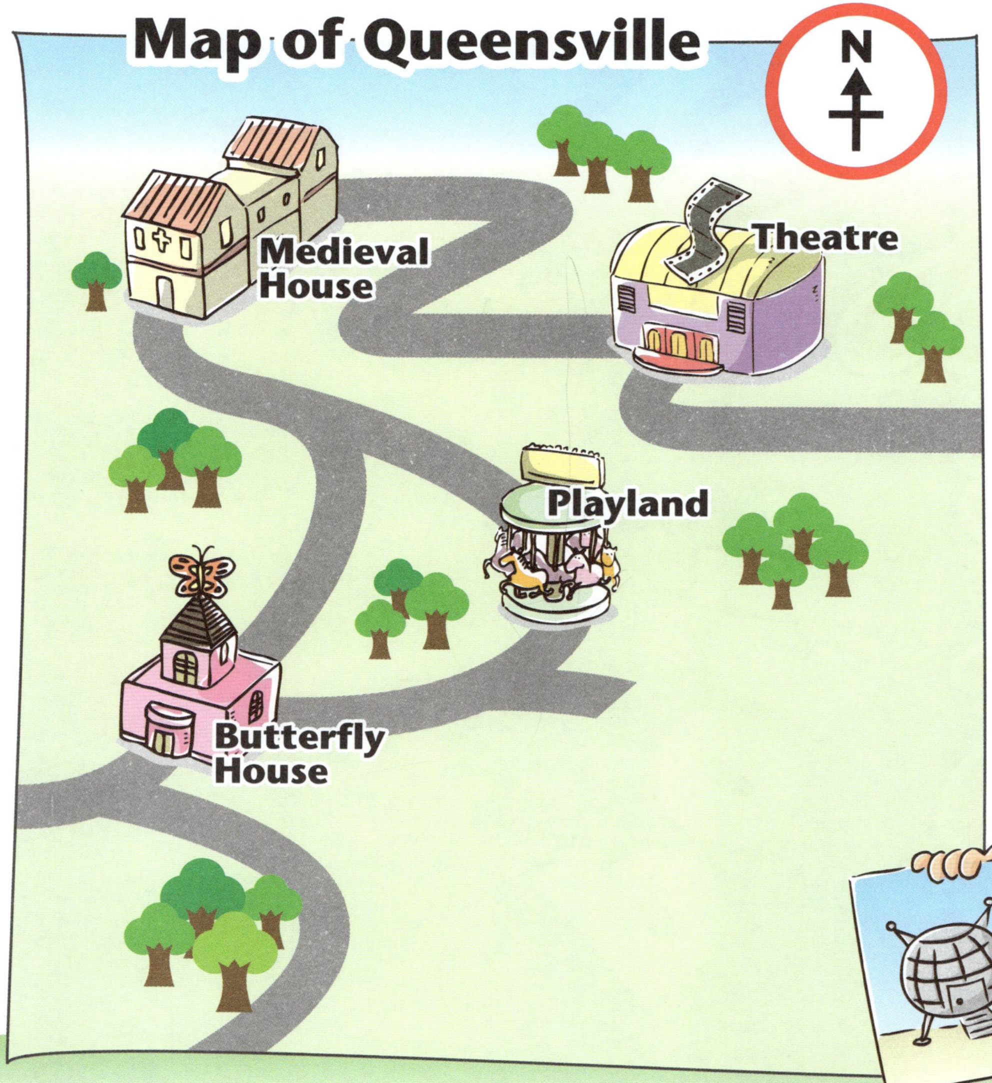

Map of Queensville

1. south of the Medieval House: Butterfly house
2. northeast of Playland: Theatre
3. northwest of Playland: _____
4.  Draw the Science Centre to the southeast of the Butterfly House.

Arts & Crafts

Materials:
- orange
- whole cloves
- large needle
- string

You'll need an adult's help with this.

Directions:

1. Roll orange on table to soften.

2. Poke sharp end of cloves into orange.

3. Thread needle with string and push through top of orange.

4. Hang in kitchen for pleasant aroma.

Sally's Day at the Theme Park

Part 1

Sally went to the theme park with her parents. But Sally could only choose one ride to go on because her family was poor.

This is hard to choose. I want to try the fairy ride.

The mermaid ride seems fun too.

I like the princess's castle!

The Big Dipper looks exciting, and the carousel turns fast.

But at last, Sally chose the ghost train.

I choose this one!

The train went into a tunnel. There were ghosts, monsters, and bats.

It was time to go home. But Sally got lost. She was locked in the park all alone.

Where am I?

To be continued...

Ontario Place

Nestled amidst the hustle and bustle of downtown Toronto, Ontario Place is a great retreat for families and is full of exciting things to do.

Hold on to your hats and get ready to scream because there are many thrilling rides in this amusement park! Want to test your courage? Try going on "Free Fall", the impressively high drop tower that will make you plummet to the ground.

There is also a water park in Ontario Place. You can dip into the pools to escape the summer heat, or go down the twisting waterslides.

If you have the chance to visit the park during the "Festival of Fire", you will be amazed by the spectacular fireworks that light up the Toronto night sky. What a perfect finish to a fun-filled summer day!

WEEK 6

English
- read a story and correct misspelled words
- create lists and new words
- match synonyms
- use plural form

Mathematics
- read a calendar
- choose appropriate measurement units
- find surface areas
- calculate the costs of objects

Science
- identify the effects of moving air
- learn the various forms of water
- identify solids and liquids, and their characteristics

Social Studies
- associate things with the corresponding countries
- explore nationalities

Arts & Crafts
- make a paper turkey

ISBN: 978-1-897457-97-9

Week 6

A. Read the story. There are eight words that are not spelled correctly. Circle them and rewrite them correctly on the lines.

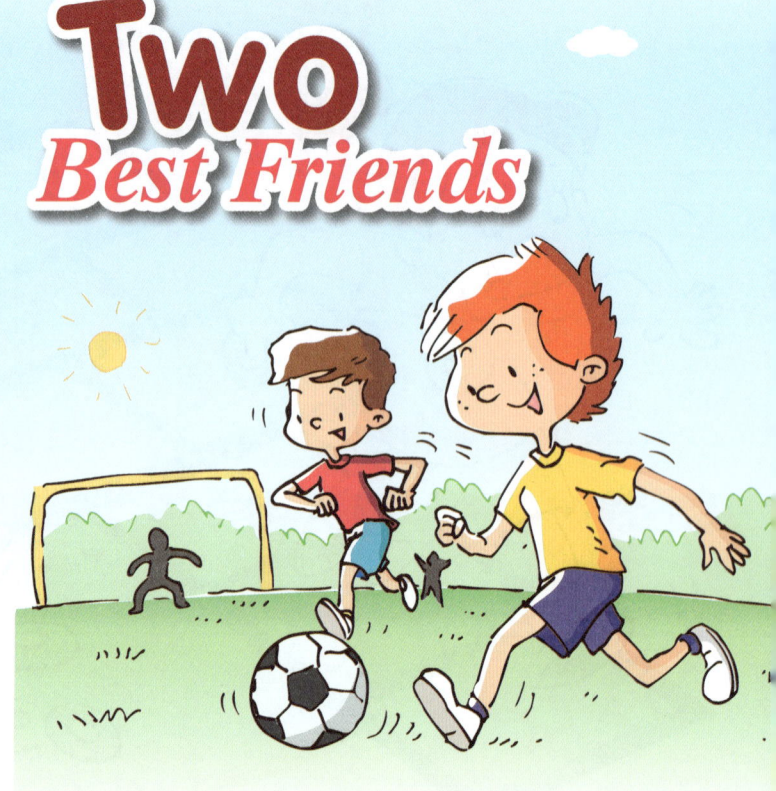

Kyle and Daniel are next door neighbours and they are also best freinds. They spend most of their free time together.

On summor days, the two boys can be found in the feild playing soccer. When the sun gets too hot, the boys clime up to the tree house where they spend their time reeding their favourite comic books. Kyle enjoys reading Spider-Man while Daniel allways picks Superman.

In wintor, both Kyle and Daniel play hockey. They are on the same teem. Kyle is the goalie and Daniel is a forward. They both hope that one day the Toronto Maple Leafs will win the Stanley Cup.

- _____
- _____
- _____
- _____
- _____
- _____
- _____
- _____

English

B. Think about your best friend. Write three things on each list.

How we are **the same**

- _____
- _____
- _____

How we are **different**

- _____
- _____
- _____

C. Write four words that you can create using the letters in the word "friendship".

Examples

end

den

dish

- _____
- _____
- _____
- _____

D. Circle the words in the word search. Then match them with the synonyms.

little   glad   toss   funny   caring   choose

a	t	n	c	h	o	o	s	e	b
v	n	g	p	m	y	q	l	w	k
b	j	l	i	t	t	l	e	i	t
n	u	a	p	r	o	h	e	q	n
h	j	d	w	n	s	e	h	n	q
f	q	e	b	n	s	k	w	t	b
u	n	a	u	j	y	o	e	b	r
n	b	c	a	r	i	n	g	n	e
n	w	g	t	z	o	l	w	t	b
y	i	h	g	y					
k	b	e							n
e	p	q							w

Synonyms

1. throw _____

2. small _____

3. amusing _____

4. pick _____

5. kind _____

6. happy _____

E. **Fill in the blanks with the plural form of each noun.**

1.

    child _____

2.

    deer _____

3. The dentist cleaned my (tooth) _____ .

4. She is scared of (mouse) _____ .

5. Six kids have twelve (foot) _____ .

6. All the (man) _____ in the band played the guitar.

7. These (moose) _____ are crossing the river.

8.

    Look! Two (goose) _____ are dancing.

A. Complete Jane's calendar. Then answer the questions.

1.

Jane's Calendar _____
the tenth month of the year

SUN	MON	TUE	WED	THU	FRI	SAT
	1	2			5	
	8		10			13
14			17	18		
21	22	23			26	
		30				

2. Halloween is on _____ (day of the week).

3. Jane's birthday is on _____ (date).

4. _____ (date) is the Sunday before Jane's birthday.

5. Jane goes to the library every Saturday. On what dates does she go to the library?

_____

B. Write the correct units (m/cm) for each item. Then record the measurements of the sticker album and check ✓ the most appropriate gift bag.

- The fishing rod is about 1 _____ long.

- The string for the kite is about 30 _____ long.

- The string of the yoyo is about 105 _____ long.

length
_____

width
_____

Gift bag for the album:

A   15 cm, 8 cm

B   5 cm, 10 cm

C   11 cm, 8 cm

C. Record the area of each sticker by counting the number of squares covered. Then answer the questions.

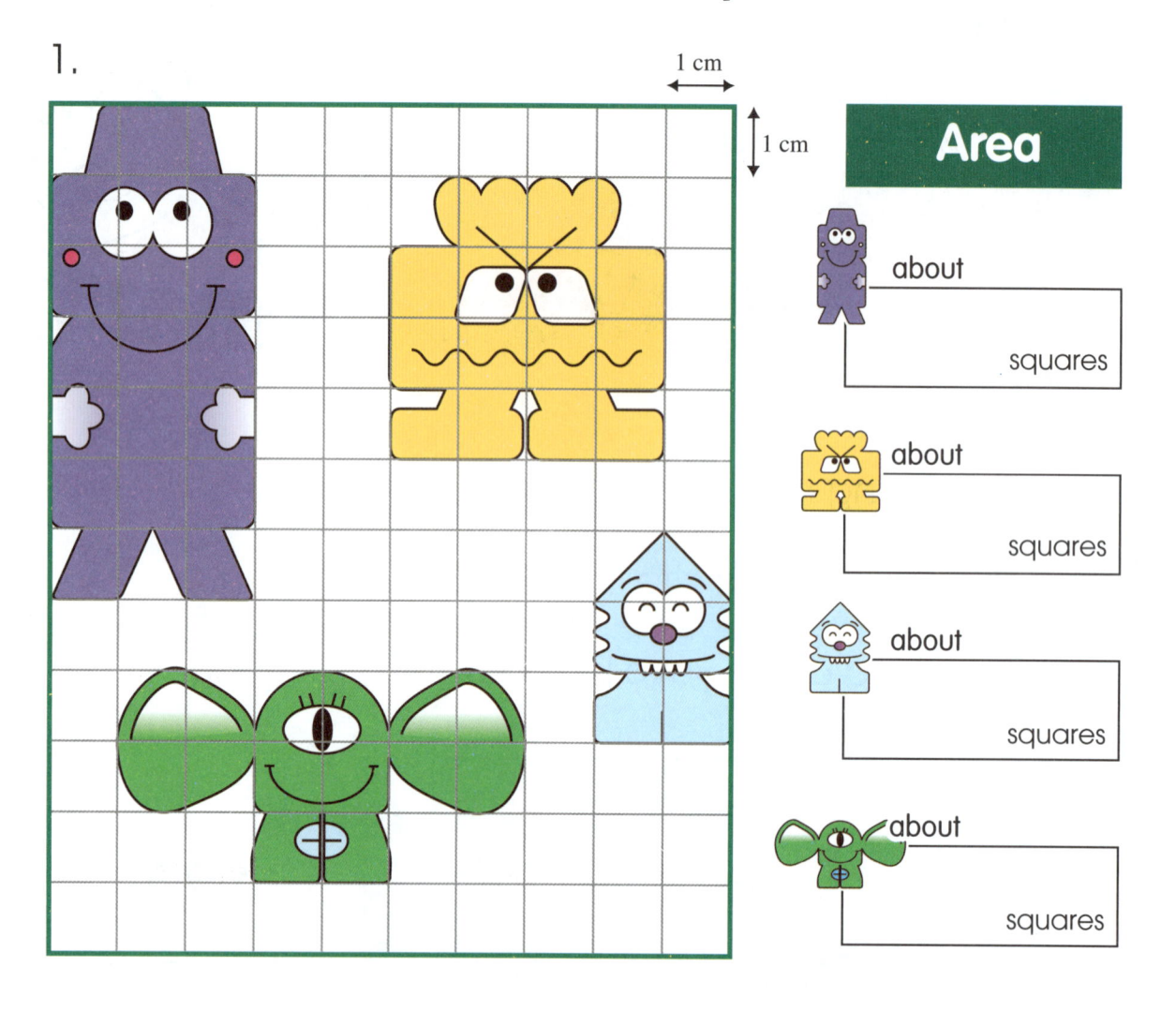

1.

Area

about _____ squares

about _____ squares

about _____ squares

about _____ squares

2a. How many 🟣 can be put on one page of the album at most?

_____

b. How many 🟡 can be put on one page of the album at most?

_____

D. Complete the table to show the costs of the stickers. Then answer the questions.

1.

Cost for	5¢	4¢	2¢	3¢
1 sticker				
2 stickers				
3 stickers				
4 stickers				
5 stickers				

2. Each pack of stickers costs 55¢. If I pay 3 quarters for a pack, what is my change?

_____

3. If I want to buy 3 stickers of each type, how much will I pay?

_____

A. Read what the woman says. Then check ✓ the pictures in which things are happening because of moving air.

Air and water are all around us wherever we go. We can't see air, but we can see what it does to things when it moves, as wind.

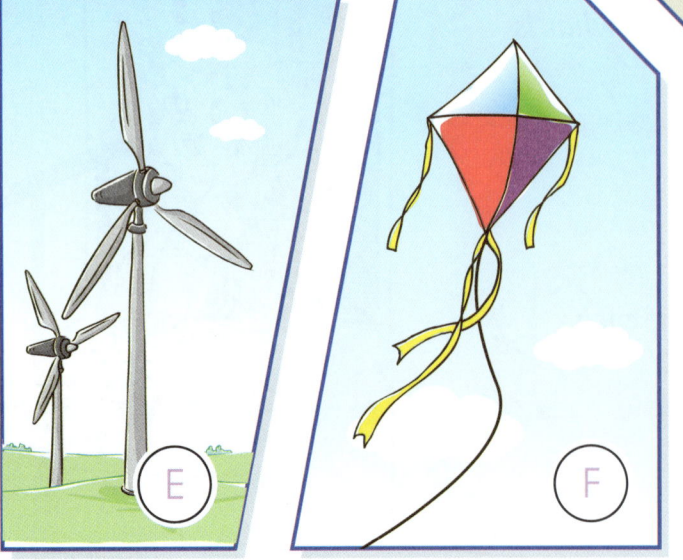

Science

B. **Circle the six water words in the word search and write them on the lines. Then match the words with the pictures.**

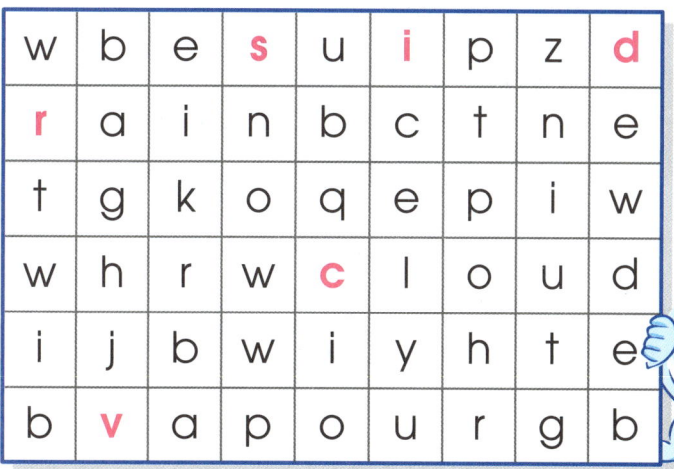

The first letter of each water word is highlighted.

Water Words

r_____ •

s_____ •

i_____ •

d_____ •

c_____ •

v_____ •

Our bodies are mostly made of water.

115

Grade 2-3

C. Identify each thing as a "solid" or "liquid". Then circle the correct words.

1.

Solid or **Liquid**

A _____
B _____
C _____
D _____
E _____
F _____

2.

liquid

- **takes / does not take** the shape of the container it is in
- **can / cannot** be poured

3.

solid

- **has / does not have** its own shape
- shape **does not change / changes** easily

Science

D. Read what Katie says. Then write the correct descriptions.

Things in Water

dissolves   sinks   floats

There are many ways solids and liquids interact with each other.

Water on Things

repelled   absorbed

1. sugar in water: _____

2. cork in water: _____

3. sand in water: _____

1. water on sock: _____

2. water on towel: _____

3. water on raincoat: _____

A. Match each picture with the country it is related to.

Italy   Mexico   China   Japan   Egypt
Holland   Australia   Canada   United States

A
B
C
D
E
F 
G
H 
I

Country

A _____   B _____   C _____

D _____   E _____   F _____

G _____   H _____   I _____

Social Studies

B. Write the nationality of each child.

1. _____
2. _____
3. _____

4. _____
5. _____
6. _____

7. _____
8. _____
9. _____

Grade 2-3

Turkey in a Bag

Materials

- paper bag
- scissors
- newspaper for stuffing
- turkey head tracer (below)
- construction paper for feathers (red, yellow, orange, brown)
- glue
- elastic band

Week 6

Arts & Crafts

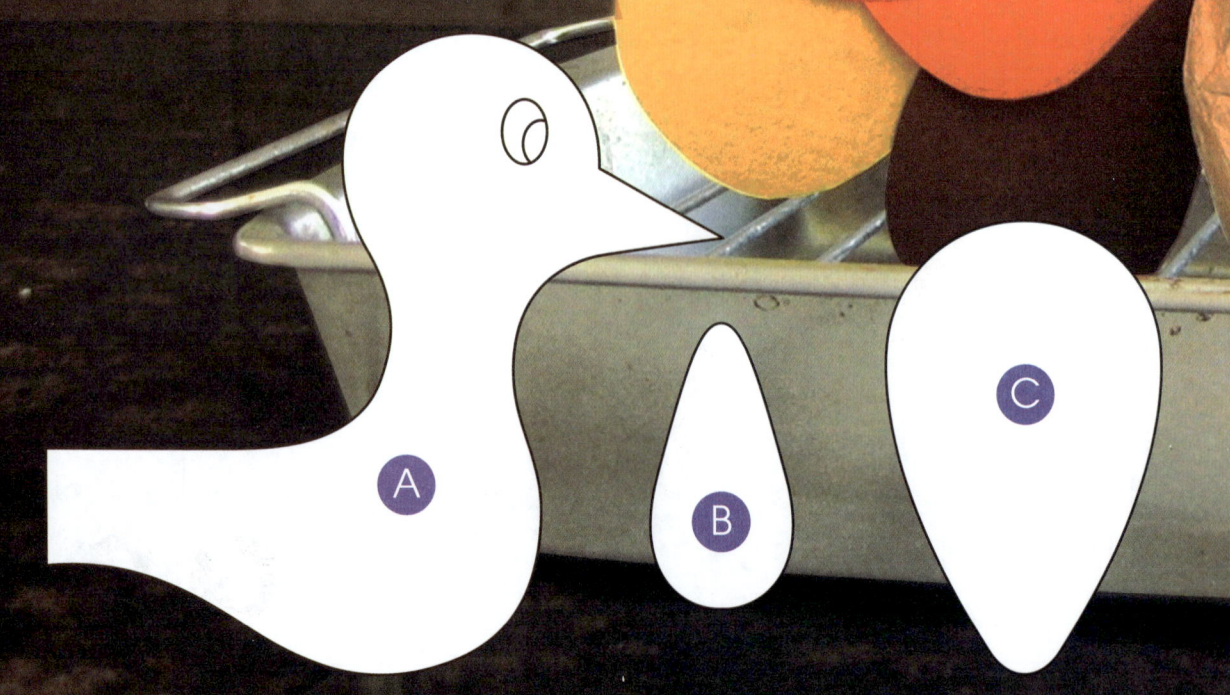

Arts & Crafts

Directions:

1. Stuff paper bag with newspaper strips.

2. Twist top closed. Secure with elastic band.

3. Draw turkey head Ⓐ on brown construction paper. Trace wattle Ⓑ from red construction paper. Glue together as shown.

4. Trace and cut feathers Ⓒ from orange, brown, red, and yellow construction paper.

5. Attach feathers to back of turkey bag and glue head in place.

Sally's Day at the Theme Park

Suddenly, a princess appeared outside the princess's castle.

Hello, Sally! Today you went on just one ride. Do you want to try more?

The mermaid took Sally on the waterslide!

Captain Fearless took Sally up and down the Big Dipper.

She rode a white horse on the carousel.

She spun round and round with the fairies.

Wake up, Sally! It's time to go home.

Sally woke up. She wondered if it was all just a dream.

Just as Sally was leaving, she saw the princess waving at her.

Thank you for the rides, Princess.

The End

A Pirate Adventure in Ottawa

Ottawa, Canada's capital city, is, as you know, home to the Parliament, our Prime Minister, and…pirates?!

Indeed, though they are not real pirates, the costumed and energetic crew of "Pirate Adventures" will give you a swashbuckling experience you'll never forget! Venture aboard their grand ship, and live the life of a pirate for a 75-minute sail along the Rideau Canal in Ottawa.

This is a journey of non-stop action and excitement! You will have the chance to read a treasure map, solve clues, and sing pirate songs. You will even be called upon to defend the ship from attackers with the water cannons on-board!

While the gentle summer breeze lifts the ship's sails, let this friendly band of pirates lead you on the adventure of a lifetime!

ISBN: 978-1-897457-97-9

Week 7

English
- read a story
- match synonyms
- write a message
- find antonyms
- choose appropriate homophones

Mathematics
- colour a pictograph
- solve problems using a pictograph
- recognize and complete patterns
- identify transformations

Science
- match simple machines with their definitions
- understand the functions of simple machines
- understand levers

Social Studies
- label parts of the globe
- know the characteristics of different regions

Arts & Crafts
- make a Chinese dragon

ISBN: 978-1-897457-97-9

A. Read the passage.

It was a hot summer day. Justin <u>strolled</u> along the shore. He was looking for <u>unusual</u> shells when suddenly he <u>noticed</u> a glass bottle floating in the water. Justin ran quickly and <u>grabbed</u> it when it came close to the shore. There was something <u>inside</u>. It was a piece of paper neatly <u>rolled</u> and tied with a ribbon. Justin <u>cautiously</u> opened the bottle and pulled out the paper. On the paper, the following was written:

A Message in a Bottle

Dear Finder,

My name is Emily and I live on beautiful Prince Edward Island. I am sending this message to tell people about my home. An ocean surrounds Prince Edward Island. I am always happy when I smell the salt water and hear the sound of the waves hitting the rocks along the shore. The beaches are a great place for building sandcastles and for finding shells. The sky is blue and filled with many birds. I love my home and hope that one day you could visit my island.

Yours truly,
Emily

B. Match each underlined word in the story with its synonym.

1. took   _____

2. curled   _____

3. walked   _____

4. strange   _____

5. carefully   _____

6. detected   _____

Synonyms are words with similar meanings.

fast
quickly

C. Write a paragraph for a bottle message describing a beautiful place that you would like to share with others.

Dear Finder,

_____

_____

_____

_____

_____

_____

                              _____

                              _____

D. **Complete the crossword puzzle with the antonyms of the words from the passage.**

Antonyms are opposites.

big
small

Clues: cold, pushed, never, slowly, carelessly, closed, outside, nothing

English

E. **Fill in the blanks with the correct homophones.**

Homophones are words that sound the same but have different spellings and meanings.

*I **write** with my **right** hand.*

1. I spent one _____ vacationing on Prince Edward Island.
   _{weak/week}

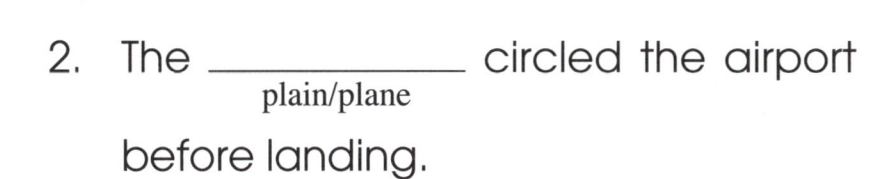

2. The _____ circled the airport before landing.
   _{plain/plane}

3. Ann wore her _____ bathing suit to the beach.
   _{new/knew}

4. I _____ enjoy a trip to an island.
   _{would/wood}

5. Sam took his boat out to the _____ .
   _{see/sea}

6. The _____ sky was filled with seagulls.
   _{blew/blue}

A. Count and colour the pictograph to show the number of biscuits in a box.

Number of Biscuits

Milk Chocolate	Dark Chocolate	Orange Flavoured	Cream Puff

Mathematics

B. **Look at the pictograph again. Then answer the questions.**

1. How many 🔺 and 🍪 are there?

   _____ biscuits

2. How many biscuits are there in all?

   _____ biscuits

3. How many biscuits are in the shape of a square?

   _____ biscuits

4. How many biscuits with 4 sides are there?

   _____ biscuits

5. All the biscuits are put equally into 4 bags. How many biscuits are there in each bag?

   _____ biscuits

6. *I paid $1 for this box of biscuits.*

   Draw coins to show her change.

   86¢

   _____ cents

131

Grade 2-3

C. See how many biscuits each child has eaten in the past three days. Follow the pattern to draw the biscuits that each child will eat on Thursday. Then circle the correct words.

1.

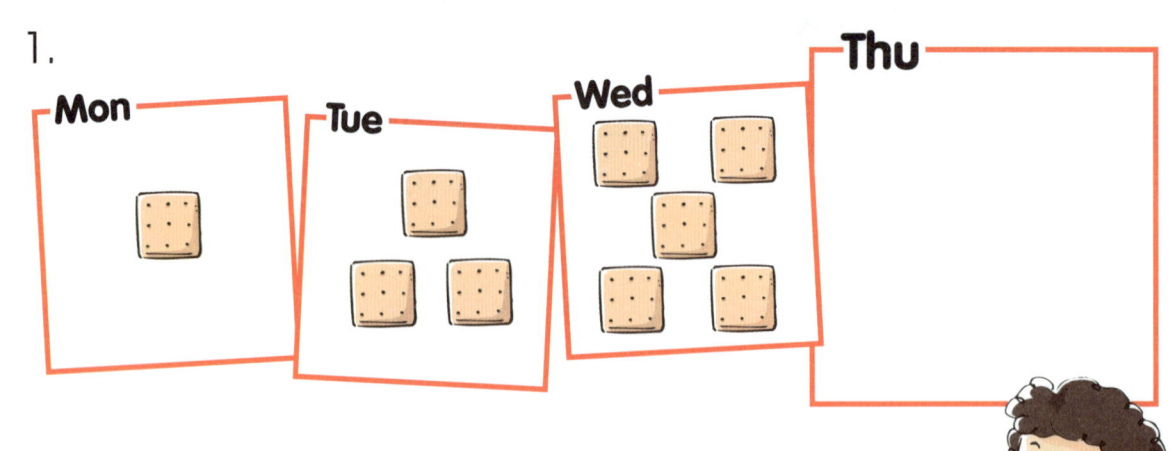

Mon — Tue — Wed — Thu

Pattern: growing / shrinking

The number of biscuits **increases** / decreases by 2 / **3** each day.

2.

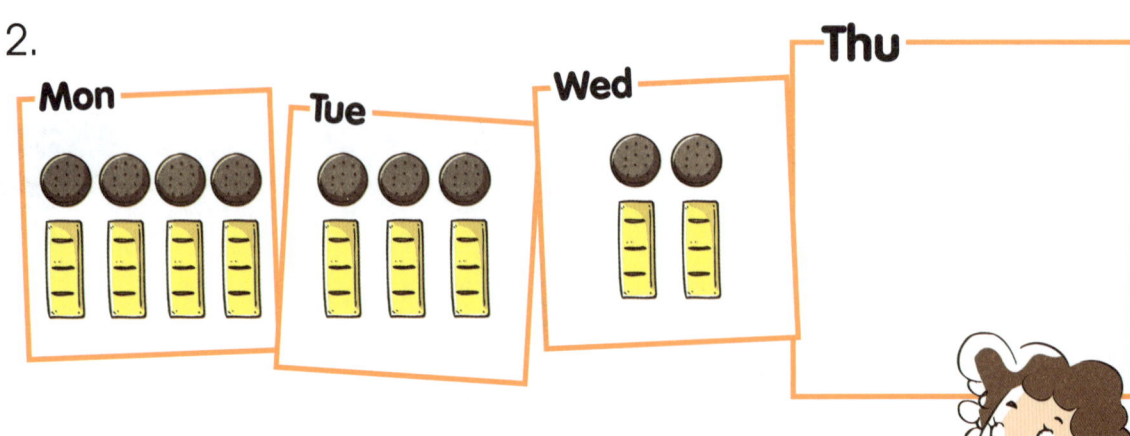

Mon — Tue — Wed — Thu

Pattern: growing / shrinking

The number of biscuits increases / **decreases** by **2** / 3 each day.

Mathematics

D. Write the correct words in the arrows to tell how each picture was moved. Then draw to answer the question.

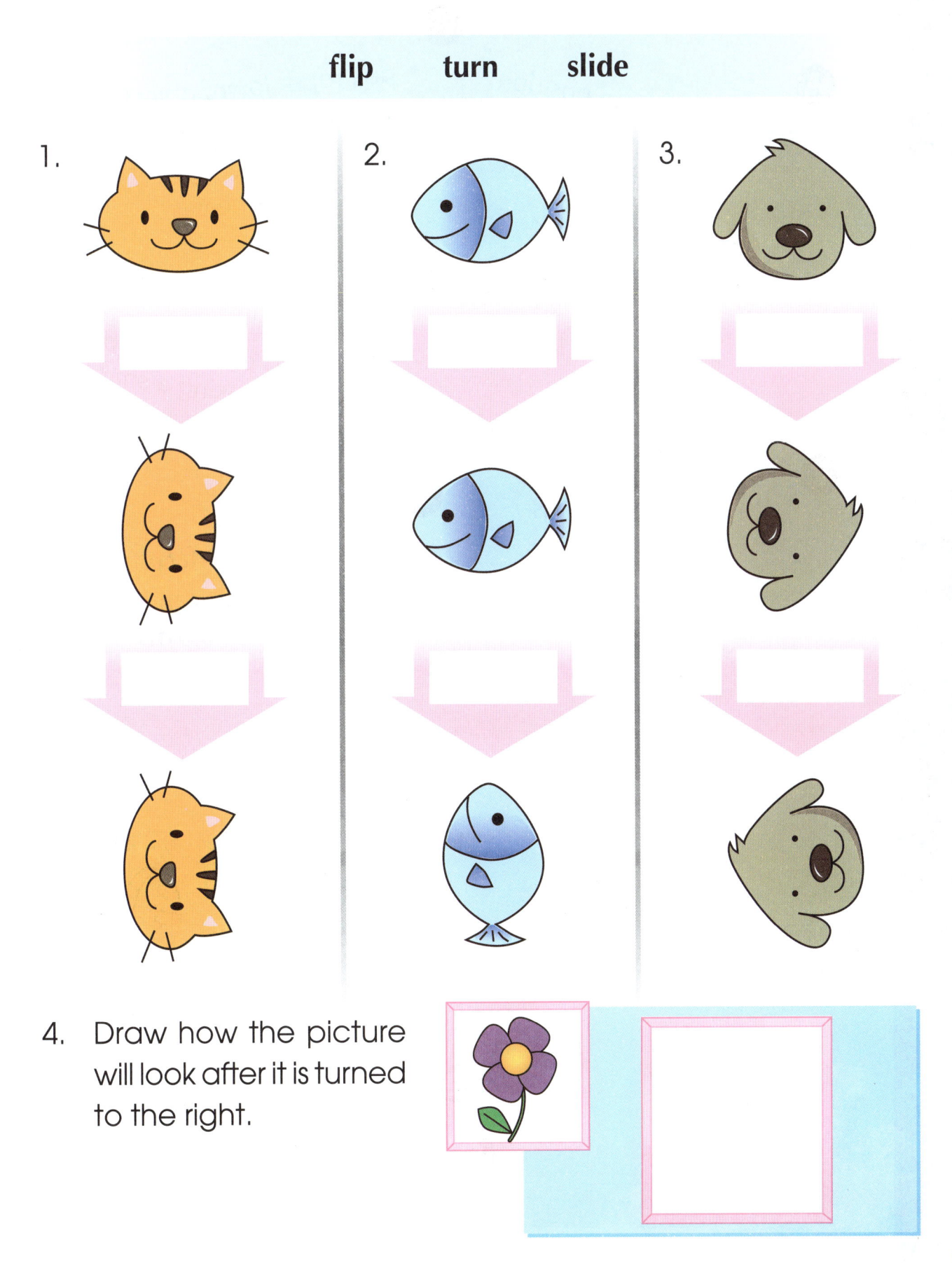

flip   turn   slide

1.

2.

3.

4. Draw how the picture will look after it is turned to the right.

A. Machines are used to make work easier. Match the clues with the machines they describe. Write the letters.

A
- keeps things in position
- holds things together

B
- pull rope down, object goes up
- found on a clothesline or a flagpole
- looks like a wheel

C
- lifts a big man
- turns on a light
- cracks a nut

D
- pencil sharpener, knife, nail
- back to back inclined planes making a sharp edge

E
- turn together
- make pulling things easier
- cars, trucks, and buses have them

F
- flat, leaning surface
- using it, things can be raised on a platform easily

Simple Machines

pulley

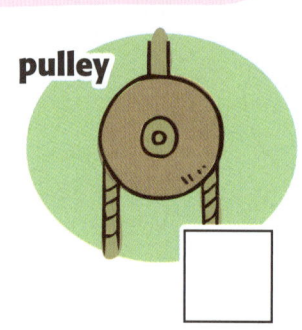

lever

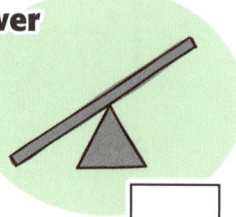

wheel and axle

wedge

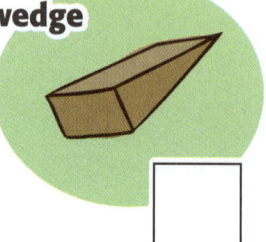

screw

inclined plane

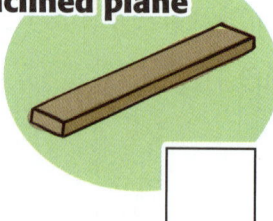

Science

Simple Machines

pulley	lever	wedge	screw	wheel and axle	inclined plane

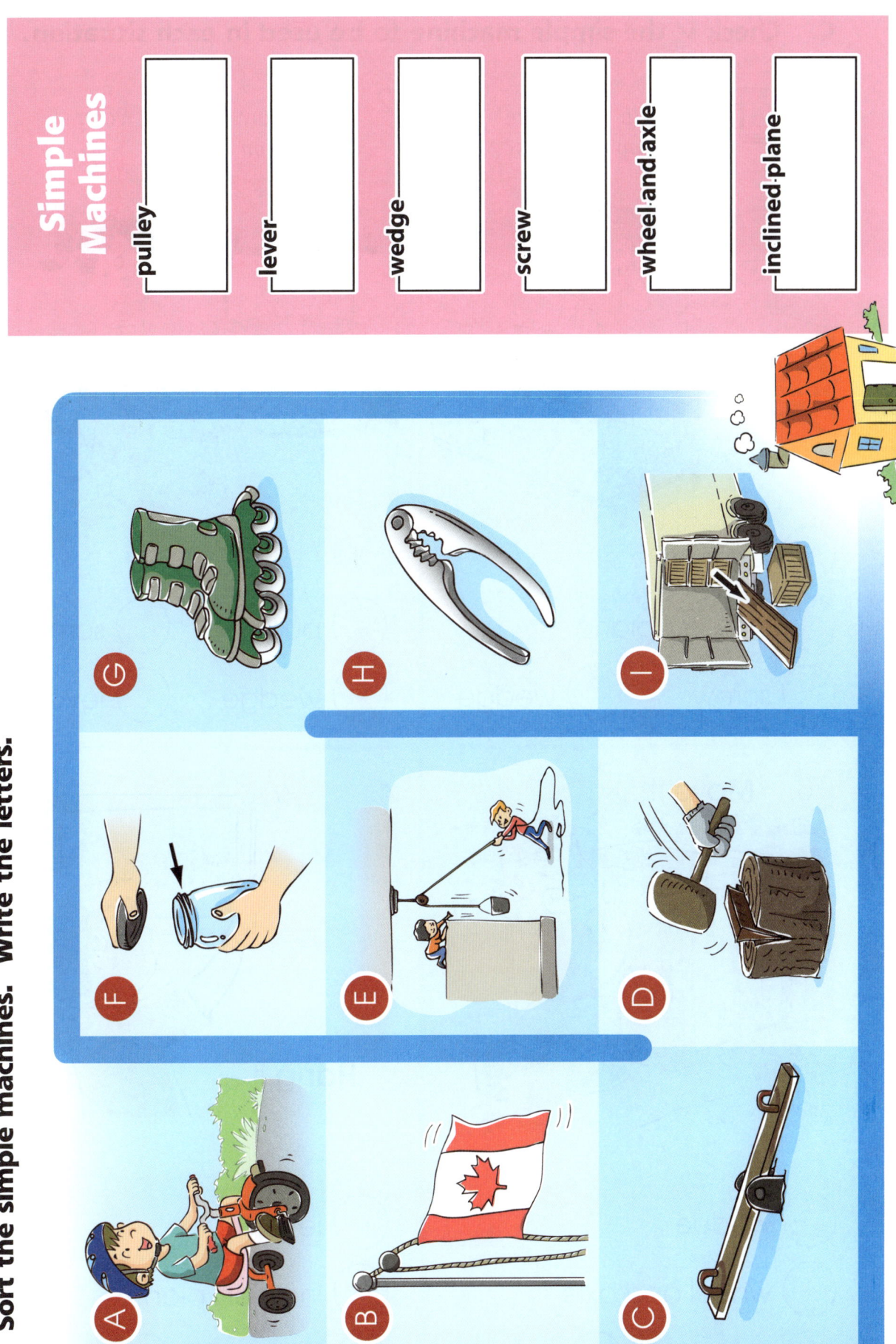

B. Sort the simple machines. Write the letters.

135

Grade 2-3

ISBN: 978-1-897457-97-9

C. Check ✔ the simple machine to be used in each situation.

1. *How do I get the couch up the stairs?*

○ lever
○ inclined plane
○ screw   ○ wedge

2. *How do I get water from the well?*

○ pulley   ○ screw
○ wedge   ○ lever

3. Move it...

○ wedge
○ wheel and axle
○ lever   ○ screw

4. Hang it...

○ lever
○ inclined plane
○ wedge   ○ screw

Science

D. For each lever, colour the arrow that correctly shows where the fulcrum is.

The **fulcrum** is the pivot point on a lever. It is the point about which a lever's arm turns.

fulcrum

137

Grade 2-3

ISBN: 978-1-897457-97-9

A. Label the globe with the given words.

**Equator   North Pole   South Pole
Southern Hemisphere   Northern Hemisphere**

Globe
A Model of the Earth

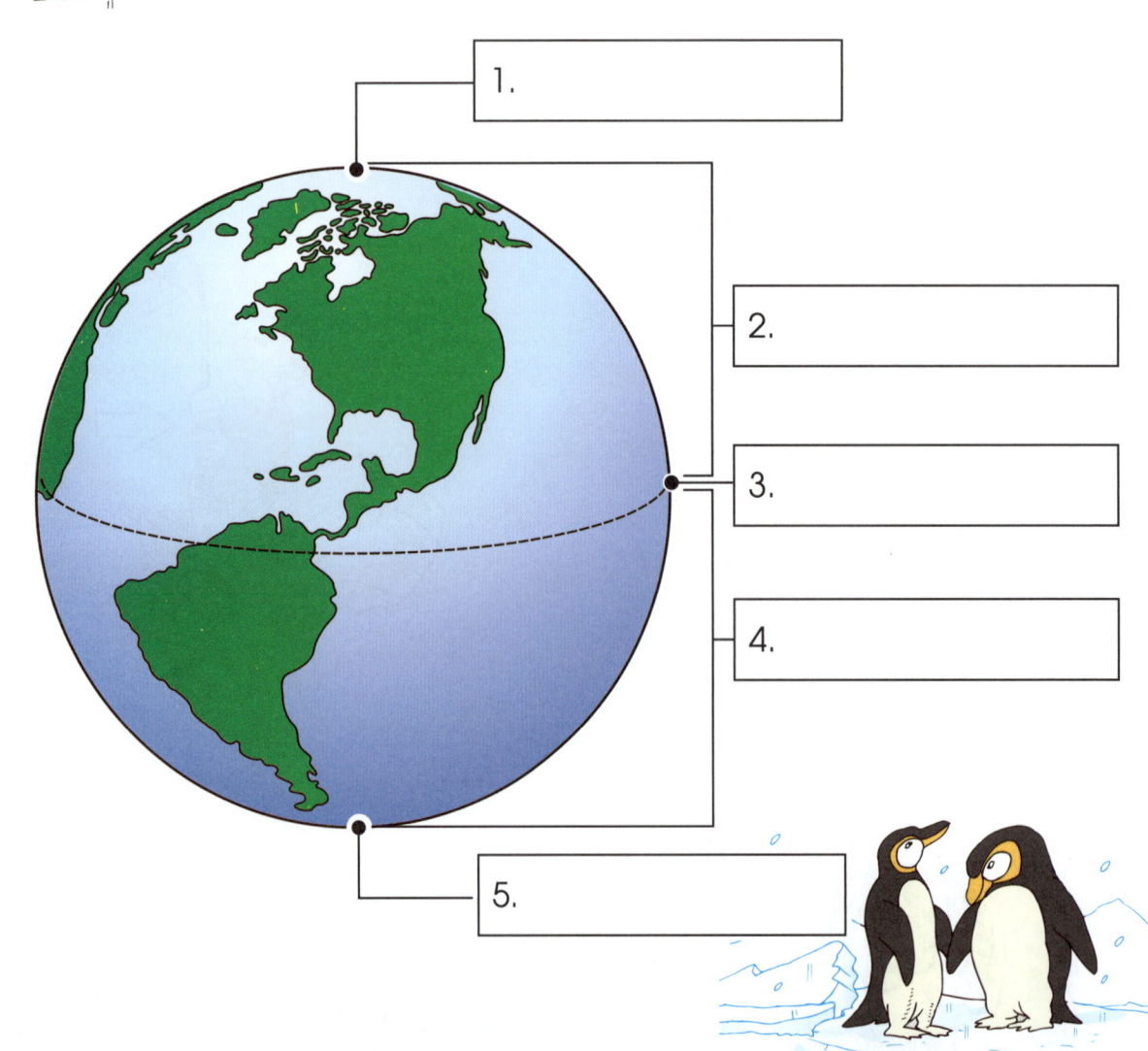

1.
2.
3.
4.
5.

B. Fill in the blanks.

1. Canada is in the _____ Hemisphere.
   _{Northern/Southern}

2. It is _____ all year round at the Equator.
   _{hot/cold}

3. It is _____ in the North Pole and the South Pole.
   _{hot/cold}

4. Part of Canada is near the _____ Pole.
   _{North/South}

5. Australia is in the _____ Hemisphere.
   _{Northern/Southern}

C. Write "T" for true and "F" for false for each statement.

1. ☐ There are four seasons in Canada.

2. ☐ Summer is the hottest season.

3. ☐ There is no snow at the Equator.

4. ☐ There are two seasons at the Equator.

5. ☐ No one lives near the North Pole.

6. ☐ It is winter in Australia when we are enjoying the summer in Canada.

CHINESE DRAGON

Week 7

Arts & Crafts

140

ISBN: 978-1-897457-97-9

Arts & Crafts

Materials:

- 1 cardboard egg carton
- paintbrush
- string
- black pipe cleaners
- glue
- paper bag
- newspaper strips
- red, orange, black, and white construction paper
- orange paint
- elastic band
- scissors

Directions:

1. Cut egg carton in half.
2. Paint it orange. Let dry.
3. Tie the two rows together with string.
4. Stuff paper bag with newspaper strips.
5. Paint bag orange. Let dry.
6. Trace parts that form the dragon head on construction paper of different colours.
7. Cut out and glue all pieces in place as shown.
8. Make two small holes below the dragon's nose and add black pipe cleaners.
9. Tie egg carton to paper bag with elastic band.
10. Glue dragon head to paper bag.

141

Grade 2-3

King Midas

Part 1

Once there was a king who lived in Greece. His name was Midas.

One day, the king found a satyr sleeping in his garden.

King Midas knew the satyr's master. He was a powerful god.

When the satyr woke up, King Midas gave him food and drinks. The satyr was very happy.

King Midas took the satyr back to his master. The thankful god gave the king one wish.

I wish everything I touch would turn to gold.

The god knew it was a bad wish. He asked King Midas to change his mind. But the king did not listen.

To be continued...

The Atlas Coal Mine

Visiting the Atlas Coal Mine near Drumheller, Alberta is a fascinating experience.

Every summer, the Atlas allows visitors to descend underground into the old mine. Unleash the explorer in you and dig into the past, as you put on a miner's hat and walk in the footsteps of a Canadian coal miner in the 1930s. As you follow the dark tunnels, you can try doing some of the miner's tasks yourself, such as raising and lowering the miner's baskets, or climbing inside coal cars!

The tour of the mine involves walking on rocky and steep ground, so make sure to wear comfortable shoes! Then, relax and enjoy the warm summer weather as you sit in a coal car and take an above-ground train tour.

A day at the Atlas is fun and educational for people of all ages!

Week 8

English
- read a story and put the events in order
- write an ending to a story
- complete a crossword puzzle
- put words in order to make sentences

Mathematics
- identify positions on a map
- calculate costs
- do addition and multiplication to solve problems
- read the time on clocks

Science
- learn and identify movements
- understand forces and the direction of movement
- do an experiment to understand friction

Social Studies
- learn about the climate of Singapore
- write about the climate where you live

Arts & Crafts
- make a milk carton birdhouse

ISBN: 978-1-897457-97-9

A. Read the story. Then put the events in order from 1 to 4.

Bottom of the Ninth

"Strike two!" yelled the umpire.

It was the bottom of the ninth inning and Kenny's team, the Sluggers, were tied with the Hurricanes. There were two outs. Kenny knew that he had to hit the ball so that his team could win the championship. He tried to stay calm but sweat kept running down his back.

Kenny squeezed the bat tightly and stared at the pitcher on the mound. The catcher was signalling to the pitcher. The pitcher was rolling the baseball around in his black mitt dreaming of a strike out. Suddenly he threw the ball. Kenny watched the ball as it came towards home plate.

◯ The score was tied between the Sluggers and the Hurricanes.

◯ The catcher was signalling to the pitcher.

◯ The pitcher suddenly threw the ball.

◯ Kenny started to sweat.

B. Write an ending to the story and give it a new title.

Your ending can be exciting, unexpected, or just plain funny.

New Title: _____

Kenny watched the ball as it came towards home plate.

_____

_____

_____

_____

_____

_____

_____

_____

The End

C. **Read the clues and complete the crossword puzzle with baseball words from the passage.**

Across

A. glove
B. He squats behind the batter.
C. The runner has to touch this to score.
D. round of game
E. where the pitcher stands

Down

1. He throws the ball.
2. club for hitting the ball
3. referee
4. being the winning team

2 across: B A S E B A L L

D. Put these words in order to make sentences. Include capital letters and periods.

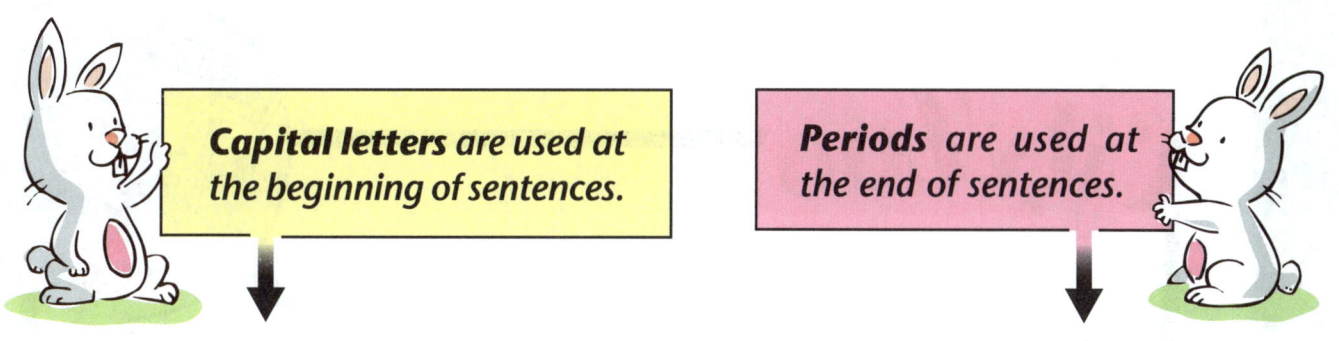

Capital letters are used at the beginning of sentences.

Periods are used at the end of sentences.

There is a baseball field beside my school.

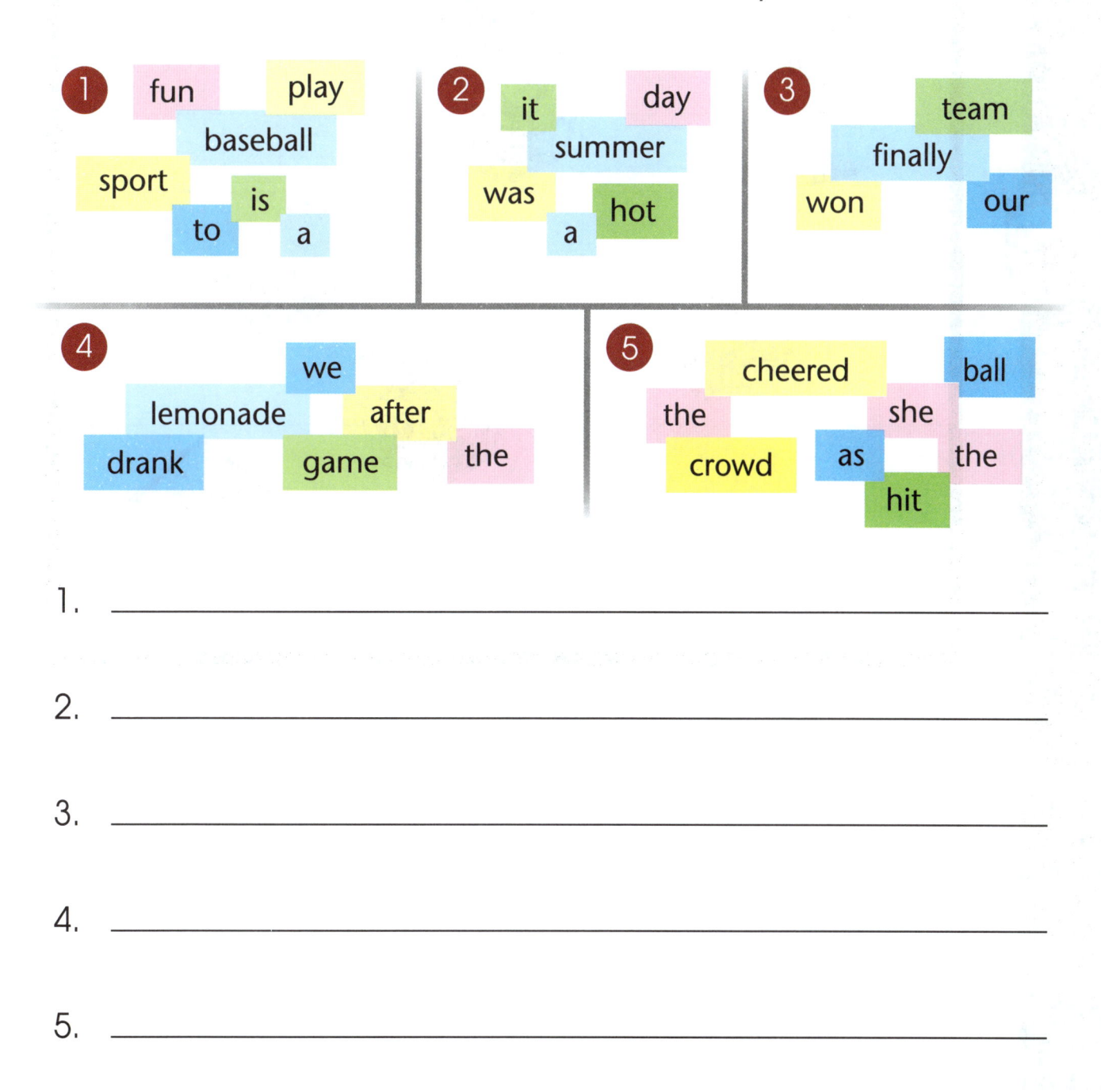

1. fun, play, baseball, sport, is, to, a

2. it, day, summer, was, hot, a

3. team, finally, won, our

4. we, lemonade, after, drank, game, the

5. cheered, ball, the, she, crowd, as, the, hit

1. _____

2. _____

3. _____

4. _____

5. _____

A. **Look at the map of the City Zoo. Help the children find their way to different spots and fill in the blanks.**

Map of the City Zoo

1. Jane wants to see the monkeys.

   She should go _____ block(s) to the _____ and

   left/right

   _____ block(s) _____ .

   up/down

2. Tim wants to see the giraffes. He should go _____

   _____ .

3. *Which way should I go from the giraffes to the Butterfly House?*

   He should go _____

   _____ .

4. *I'm watching the tigers. If I go 2 blocks to the right and 2 blocks up, what will I see?*

   She will see _____ .

5. *If an adult pays $50 for a ticket, how much is the change?*

   _____ ◯ _____ = _____

   The change is $ _____ .

   The City Zoo
   Admission
   Adults $28
   Children $16

6. How much do the tickets for two children cost?

   _____ ◯ _____ = _____

   The tickets cost $ _____ .

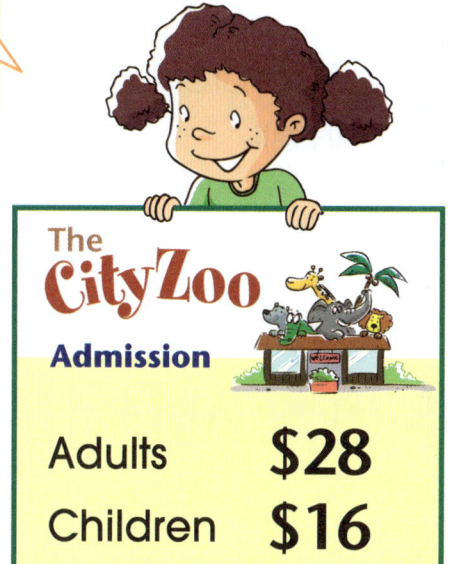

B. **Draw the pictures and fill in the missing numbers to solve the problems.**

Each child has...

| 2 🍌 to feed monkeys. | 3 🥛 of grain to feed giraffes. | 5 🍃 to feed elephants. |

1

5 children have _____ 🍌 in all.

2

4 children have _____ 🥛 in all.

3

3 children have _____ 🍃 in all.

Mathematics

C. **Help Jack write the arrival time at different spots. Then answer the questions.**

1.

a.

b.

c.

d.

2. Jack left home at 10:45 a.m. to go to the zoo. How long did it take him to get there?

_____

3. The zoo opens at 10:00 a.m. and closes at 8:00 p.m. For how many hours is it open?

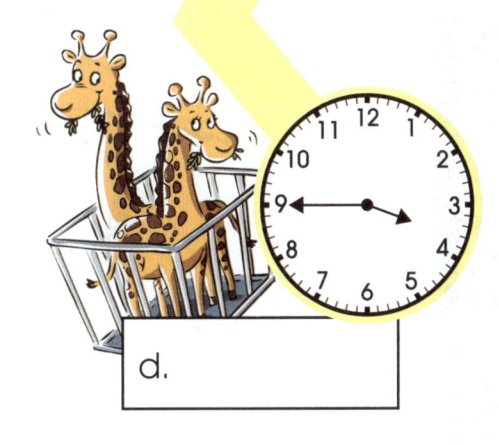

_____

4. Jack spent 30 minutes at the Butterfly House. What time did he leave the House? Draw the clock hands to show the time.

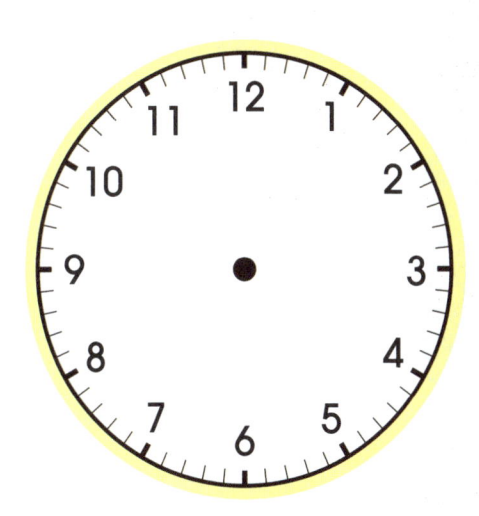

A. Circle the word that describes each movement.

spinning

sliding

rolling

swinging

turning

swinging

bouncing

sliding

swinging   rolling

Science

B. Label the movements with the given words.

Movement
sliding   bouncing   rolling
turning   swinging   spinning

Outdoor...

Movement is important in our lives and happens in different ways.

1.  _____   2.  _____   3. _____

Indoor...

4.  _____   5.   _____   6. _____

C. Trace the arrow to show the direction of movement in each case. Then write whether each object is being "pushed" or "pulled" and answer the question.

Push or Pull

Movement only happens if a force is acting on an object or body. A force can be a push or a pull.

1. apple _____

2. boy _____

3. table _____

4. Which objects in the pictures above are moving because of gravity?

_____

Gravity pulls on all things on Earth.

D. Try the experiment. Record your findings and fill in the blanks.

Friction
works in the opposite direction of the force of push or pull. Friction therefore slows down and resists movement.

Record

carpet: _____ cm

wooden floor: _____ cm

rubber mat: _____ cm

The _____ provided the most friction.

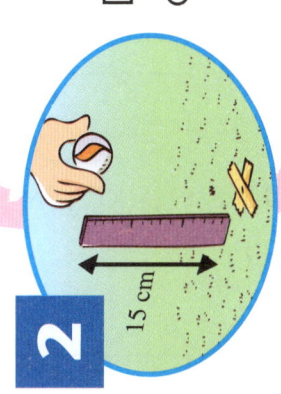

Step

1 Mark a cross on the carpet with tape.

2 Drop a marble 15 cm above the cross.

3 Measure the distance the marble travelled from the cross. Do the recording. Then repeat the steps on the wooden floor and rubber mat.

Read the postcard. Then answer the questions.

Hi Jason,

We're having a good time here in Singapore.

Singapore is close to the Equator. It is hot all year round and it rains quite a lot, too. I always put on a T-shirt and shorts. They say there are no seasons in Singapore.

Dad's friend shows us around. I've tried fresh coconut juice. I've even tasted durians. They have a strong smell.

Yesterday, we had a fresh seafood dinner on the beach. I enjoyed the chilli crabs and prawns the most.

Will see you again in a week's time.

Your buddy,
Matt

1. Why can't coconuts or durians grow in Canada?

   _____

2. How do you know that Singapore must be close to the sea?

   _____

Social Studies

3. Why is Singapore hot all year round?

_____

_____

4. One of the crosses on the globe shows where Singapore is. Write "Singapore" beside that cross.

To: Jason Mclead
19 Apple Creek,
Toronto, Ontario
Canada

5. Write about the climate in the part of Canada where you live. Name one fun thing you can do there.

_____

_____

159

Grade 2-3

Milk Carton

Week 8

Arts & Crafts

Directions:

1. Rub carton with sandpaper.
2. Tape opening at top.
3. Paint all over milk carton.
4. Paint popsicle sticks. Let dry.
5. Cut a hole about 4 cm wide and 4 cm from bottom of carton.
6. Make 3 slits below hole. Poke popsicle sticks about half their length into slits.
7. Poke a small drainage hole in bottom of the carton and 2 at the top on the sides for ventilation.
8. Tie string through top.
9. Fill with birdseed. Hang.

ISBN: 978-1-897457-97-9

Arts & Crafts

BIRDHOUSE

Materials:

- paintbrush
- scissors
- coloured paint
- sharp knife (an adult to help)
- 500 mL milk carton
- 2 or 3 popsicle sticks
- heavy masking tape
- string
- sandpaper

An adult will need to help you with this.

Grade 2-3

King Midas

Part 2

This is wonderful!

King Midas got his wish. He touched a stone and it turned to gold.

I can't eat or drink anything!

The king was very excited. He touched everything in his palace. All of it turned to gold.

The king was hungry. But when he picked up some food, it turned to gold too.

The princess visited her father. She bent down to give him a kiss.

No, stop!

But it was too late. The princess had turned to gold.

King Midas was very sad. He went to the god.

Please take back my wish.

The god felt sorry for King Midas. He told him to wash away the wish in the river.

I'm sorry. I'll never be greedy again.

King Midas did as he was told and washed the wish away. His daughter came back to life again.

The End

The Radium Hot Springs

This summer, brave the rapids of the Kootenay River in British Columbia by going whitewater rafting!

From Radium Hot Springs, B.C., you will begin an adventure that will get your heart racing. Whitewater rafting involves paddling through thunderous waters on an inflatable boat with a group of people and a guide. So strap on your life jackets and prepare to be jostled around by the roaring rapids as you make your way along the Kootenay. The feeling is exhilarating!

This experience is also breathtaking because of the natural beauty of the area. Take the time to appreciate the beauty of the wilderness and the Canadian Rockies. You can even try to spot some wildlife!

Afterwards, why not take a swim in a hot spring? It would be a nice, relaxing end to a thrilling summer day.

SAFETY RULES

ISBN: 978-1-897457-97-9

Camping

A Dispose of trash properly.

B Dress yourself in long-sleeved shirts and wear pants.

C Wear sunscreen, a hat, and sunglasses.

D Apply bug spray frequently.

E Pitch your tent on a level site and away from the campfire.

F Do not eat anything found in the forest or field.

G If a bear wanders, tell an adult and slowly back away. If a bear charges, roll into a ball and play dead.

ISBN: 978-1-897457-97-9

Match the rules with the pictures. Write the letters.

Safety Rules

Grade 2-3

Circle the correct words.

Barbecue in an **open / indoor** space.

Make sure the barbecue is at least **3 metres / 3 centimetres** from windows and doors.

Backyard Barbecuing

Always / Never pour water into a grease fire – this will cause the flame to flare up.

It's a good idea to keep some water around for emergency use.

If you do burn yourself, run the affected area under **hot / cool** water for five minutes. If it is serious, seek medical attention immediately.

Keep the barbecue away from **trees / flowers** with low branches.

Stay **away from / close to** a hot grill and the area surrounding an ignited barbecue.

At a Beach

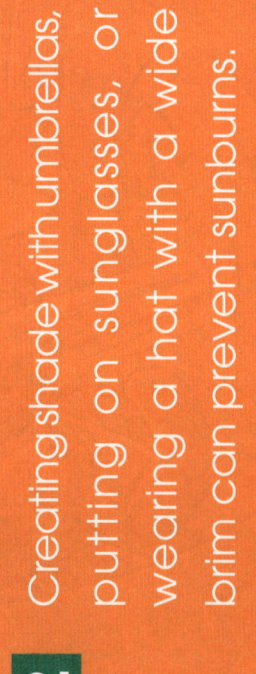

1. Apply sunscreen on all exposed parts of the body.

2. Creating shade with umbrellas, putting on sunglasses, or wearing a hat with a wide brim can prevent sunburns.

3. Always stay with an adult.

4. Swim only in designated areas.

Safety Rules

Colour the people's skin light brown to help them apply sunscreen.

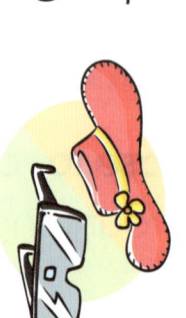

Tim is playing with his mom in the water. Draw Tim's mom.

Give Kevin a pair of sunglasses and Judy a hat with a wide brim.

Tim's dad is swimming in the designated area. Draw Tim's dad.

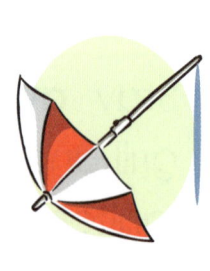

Give Mrs. White an umbrella.

ISBN: 978-1-897457-97-9

Safety Rules

Mrs. White

Judy

Kevin

Tim

Draw or colour to keep the people safe.

171

Grade 2-3

ISBN: 978-1-897457-97-9

Rock Climbing

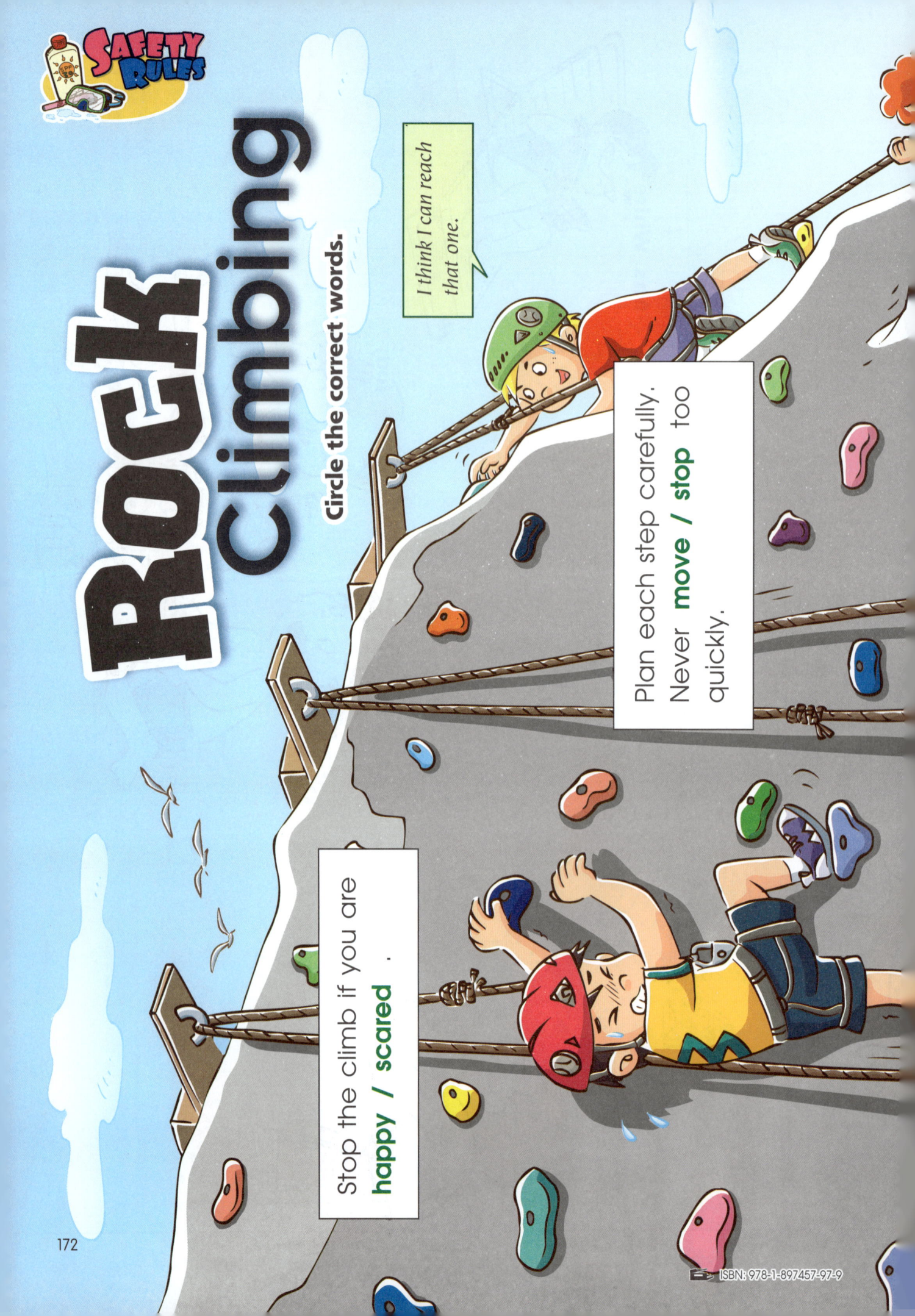

Circle the correct words.

I think I can reach that one.

Plan each step carefully. Never **move / stop** too quickly.

Stop the climb if you are **happy / scared**.

Safety Rules

Wear a **cap / helmet** and make sure it is secure.

Wear shoes that **grip / slide** well.

Always keep your climbing equipment **securely / randomly** fastened.

Do not look too far down, as it may make you **nervous / prudent**.

Don't worry. You can try putting your left hand on the yellow one.

Listen to / Ignore the instructions at all times.

The Water Park

SAFETY RULES

Match the pictures with the correct descriptions. Write the letters in the circles. Then paste the lifeguard in the box.

A If you cannot swim, wear a life jacket.

B Before you start going down a waterslide, get into the correct position: face up and feet first.

C Always swim with a buddy; never swim alone.

D Never get on the waterslide when someone is on it.

E Apply sunblock frequently to avoid sunburn.

Safety Rules

175

Grade 2-3

ISBN: 978-1-897457-97-9

ISBN: 978-1-897457-97-9

GRADE 2-3

Social Studies

A. home ; hearts ; strong ; land ; guard
B. (Trace and colour.)
C ; B ; A

Week 5

English

B. 1. She decided to set up a stand in her front yard and sell watermelon slices.
   2. Lester's lemonade stand was taking away all of Wilma's business.
   3. Lester's sign was beautiful.
   (Individual drawing)
C. (Draw a line through these sentences.)
   1. Some fruits are seedless.
   2. There are four people in Kate's family.
   3. Mary loves to write poetry.
D. 1. it's
   2. who's
   3. she'll
   4. it'll
   5. I've
   6. they've
   7. you are
   8. will not
   9. that is
   10. are not
   11. does not
   12. were not
   I haven't sold a single slice of watermelon, so I'll make a big sign for my stand.

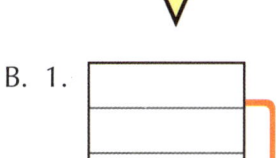

Mathematics

A. 1. cone ; cube ; cylinder ; rectangular prism
   2. 
   3. 
   4.

B. 1. 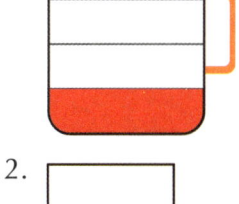
   2. 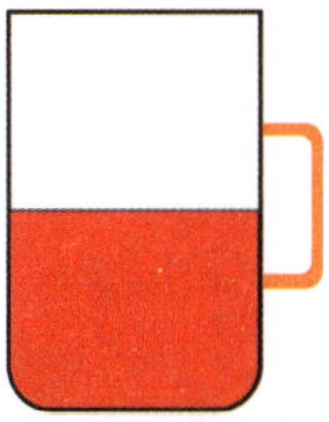
   3.

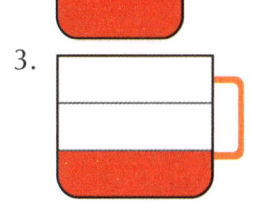

C. 1.  $\frac{2}{6}$; $\frac{2}{6}$ 2. $\frac{4}{8}$; $\frac{1}{8}$
   3. $\frac{7}{9}$; $\frac{1}{9}$ 4. $\frac{1}{7}$; $\frac{4}{7}$

D.

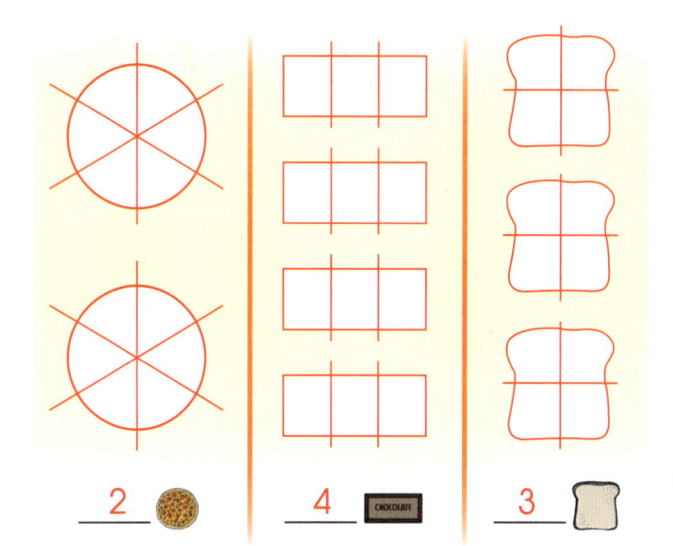

2   4   3

ANSWERS

E. 1. top
   2. A
   3. Spinner B gives you an equal chance of getting one of the three prizes. With spinner A, you are more likely to get a top.

Science

A. 1. solid
   2. gas
   3. liquid
B. 1. solid   2. gas
   3. gas   4. liquid
   5. liquid   6. solid
C. 1. vapour   2. air
   3. water   4. condenses
   5. is heated
D. Results of the Experiment: (Individual results)
   (Suggested answers)
   1. The water level went down.
   2. The water evaporated slowly.
   3. The water went into the air.

Social Studies

A. (matching diagram)

B. 1. Butterfly House
   2. Theatre
   3. Medieval House

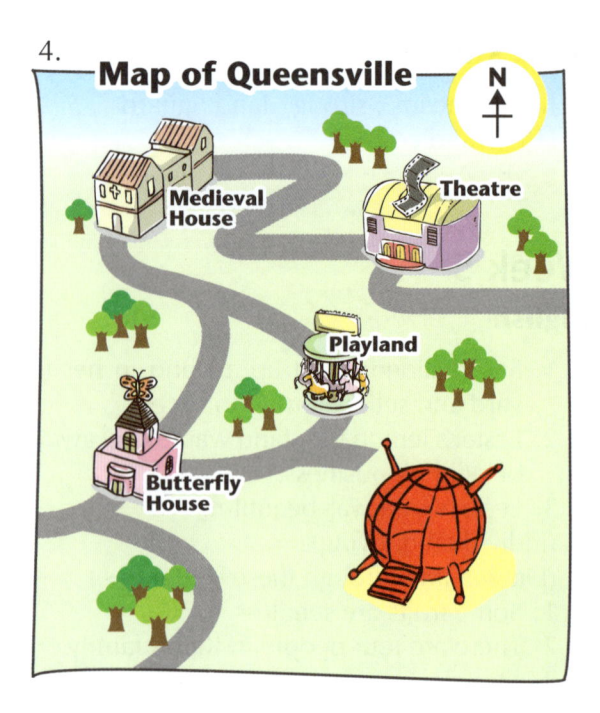

4. Map of Queensville (illustration)

Week 6

English

A. (Circle these misspelled words.)
   freinds ; summor ; feild ; clime ; reeding ; allways ; wintor ; teem
   Correct spellings:
   friends ; summer ; field ; climb ; reading ; always ; winter ; team
B. (Individual answers)
C. (Suggested answers)
   ship ; send ; fried ; ride
D.

a	t	n	c	h	o	o	s	e	b
v	n	g	p	m	y	q	l	w	k
b	j	l	i	t	t	l	e	i	t
n	u	a	p	r	o	h	e	q	n
h	j	d	w	n	s	e	h	n	q
f	q	e	b	n	s	k	w	t	b
u	n	a	u	j	y	o	e	b	r
n	b	c	a	r	i	n	g	n	e
n	w	g	t	z	o	l	w	t	b
y	i	h	g	y					
k	b	e							
e	p	q							

1. toss
2. little
3. funny
4. choose
5. caring
6. glad

E. 1. children
2. deer
3. teeth
4. mice
5. feet
6. men
7. moose
8. geese

Mathematics

A. 1.

2. Wednesday
3. October 16
4. October 14
5. on October 6, October 13, October 20, and October 27

B. m ; m ; cm ; 10 cm ; 7 cm
   Check: C

C. 1. 19 ; 14 ; 5 ; 12
   2a. 3   b. 2

D. 1.

Cost for	5¢	4¢	2¢	3¢
1 sticker	5¢	4¢	2¢	3¢
2 stickers	10¢	8¢	4¢	6¢
3 stickers	15¢	12¢	6¢	9¢
4 stickers	20¢	16¢	8¢	12¢
5 stickers	25¢	20¢	10¢	15¢

2. 20 cents
3. 42 cents

Science

A. A ; B ; E ; F

B.

w	b	e	s	u	i	p	z	d
r	a	i	n	b	c	t	n	e
t	g	k	o	q	e	p	i	w
w	h	r	w	c	l	o	u	d
i	j	b	w	i	y	h	t	e
b	v	a	p	o	u	r	g	b

Water Words

r __ain__
s __now__
i __ce__
d __ew__
c __loud__
v __apour__

C. 1. A: solid
      B: liquid
      C: solid
      D: liquid
      E: solid
      F: liquid
   2. takes ; can
   3. has ; does not change

D. Things in Water:
   1. dissolves
   2. floats
   3. sinks
   Water on Things:
   1. absorbed
   2. absorbed
   3. repelled

ANSWERS

Social Studies

A. A: China   B: Holland
    C: Mexico   D: Canada
    E: United States   F: Egypt
    G: Italy   H: Australia
    I: Japan

B. 1. American   2. Jamaican
    3. Brazilian   4. Greek
    5. Iranian   6. Indian
    7. Chinese   8. Japanese
    9. Australian

Week 7

English

B. 1. grabbed
   2. rolled
   3. strolled
   4. unusual
   5. cautiously
   6. noticed

C. (Individual writing)

D. Crossword:
- never / carelessly: CAUTIOUSLY
- cold: HO / ALWAYS
- closed: OPENED
- outside: INSIDE
- nothing: SOMETHING
- slowly: QUICKLY
- pushed: PULLED

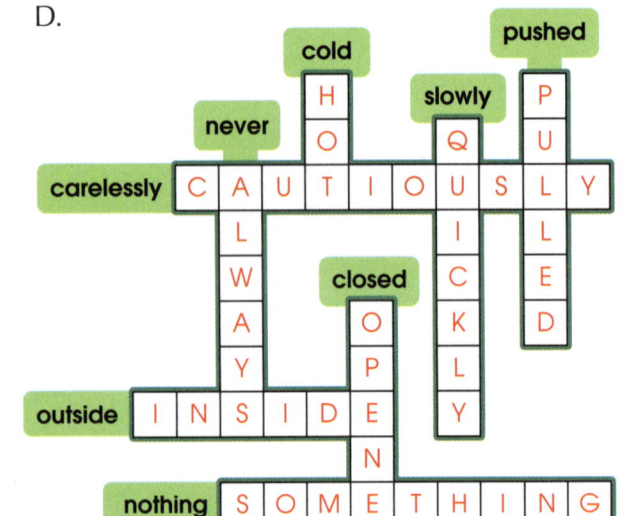

E. 1. week
   2. plane
   3. new
   4. would
   5. sea
   6. blue

Mathematics

A.

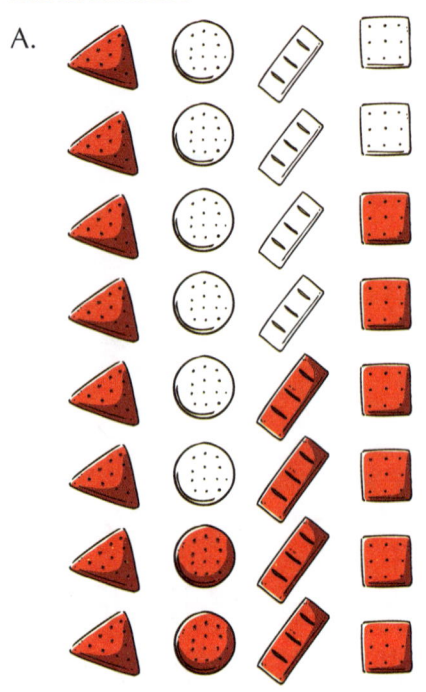

B. 1. 10   2. 20
   3. 6   4. 10
   5. 5
   6. 10¢, 1¢, 1¢, 1¢, 1¢ — 14 cents

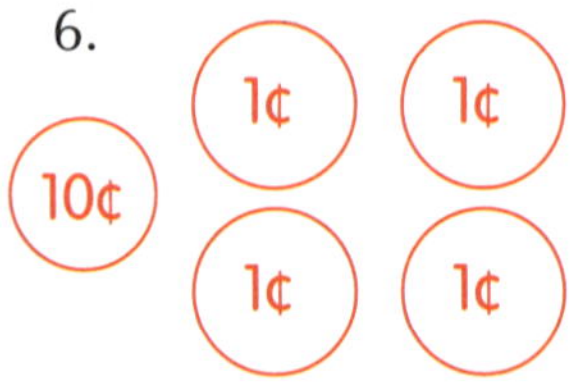

C. 1. growing ; increases ; 2
   2. shrinking ; decreases ; 2

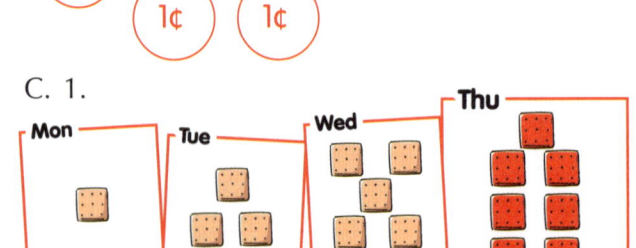

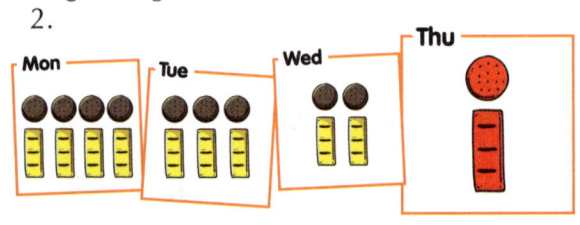

D. 1. turn ; slide
   2. slide ; turn
   3. turn ; flip

GRADE 2-3

4.

Science

A. pulley: B
   lever: C
   wheel and axle: E
   wedge: D
   screw: A
   inclined plane: F
B. pulley: B, E
   lever: C, H
   wedge: D
   screw: F
   wheel and axle: A, G
   inclined plane: I
C. 1. inclined plane   2. pulley
   3. wheel and axle   4. screw
D.

Social Studies

A. 1. North Pole
   2. Northern Hemisphere
   3. Equator
   4. Southern Hemisphere
   5. South Pole

B. 1. Northern   2. hot
   3. cold   4. North
   5. Southern
C. 1. T   2. T
   3. T   4. F
   5. F   6. T

Week 8

English

A. 1 ; 3 ; 4 ; 2
B. (Individual writing)
C.

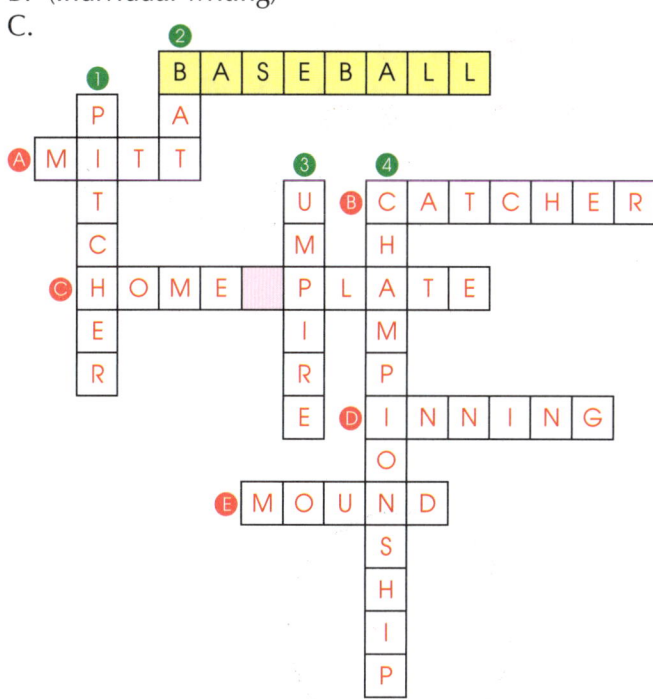

D. 1. Baseball is a fun sport to play.
   2. It was a hot summer day.
   3. Our team finally won. / Our team won finally.
   4. We drank lemonade after the game.
   5. The crowd cheered as she hit the ball.

Mathematics

A. 1. 3 ; left ; 2 ; down
   2. 1 block to the left and 3 blocks up
   3. 8 blocks to the right and 5 blocks down
   4. the elephants
   5. 50 − 28 = 22 ; 22
   6. 16 + 16 = 32 ; 32

189

Grade 2-3

B.

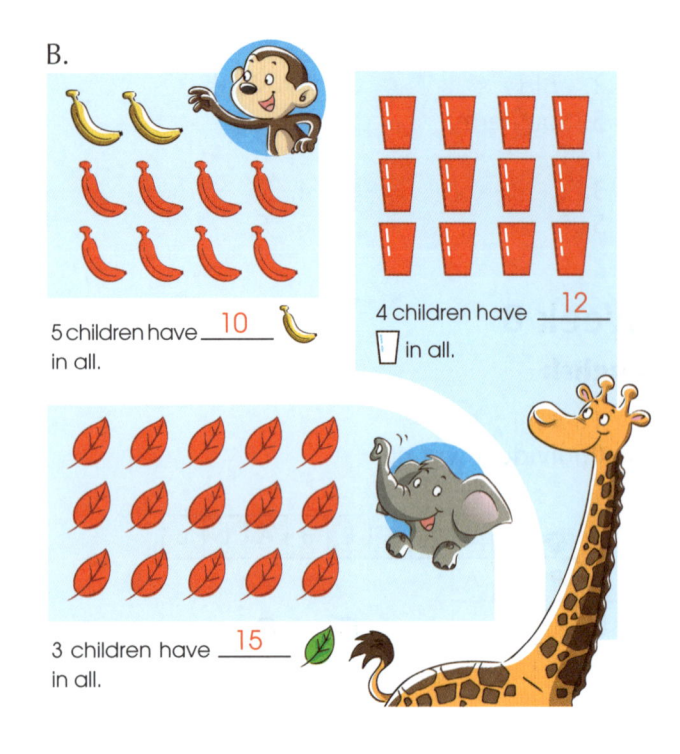

5 children have __10__ in all.

4 children have __12__ in all.

3 children have __15__ in all.

C. 1a. 11:15 a.m.
   b. 1:45 p.m.
   c. 2:30 p.m.
   d. 3:45 p.m.
2. 30 minutes
3. 10 hours
4.

Science

A. toilet paper: rolling
   fan: spinning
   faucet: turning
   clock: swinging
   ball: bouncing
B. 1. bouncing
   2. sliding
   3. swinging
   4. rolling
   5. spinning
   6. turning

C. (Trace the arrows.)
   1. pulled
   2. pulled
   3. pushed
   4. the apple and the boy
D. (Individual results)

Social Studies

1. The climate in Canada is too cold.
2. Matt can eat fresh seafood on the beach.
3. Singapore is hot all year round because it is close to the Equator.
4.

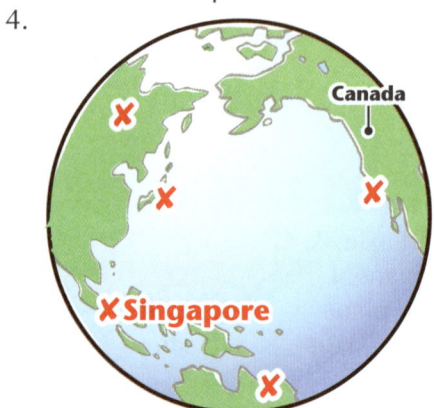

5. (Individual answer)

My Own Door Hanger

Hands-on

Trace the dotted lines. Write a message on the line. Then cut it out and hang it on your bedroom door.

- Please Do not Disturb.
- A Princess Sleeps Here.
- Please Remove Your Shoes.
- Welcome!
- Stay Out!
- Shh!
- Come In.

191

Grade 2-3

ISBN: 978-1-897457-97-9

ISBN: 978-1-897457-97-9

My Beautiful Flower

Follow the steps to make a beautiful flower.

1. Cut out A.
2. Calculate and find the petals with the answers.
3. Cut out the petals.
4. Glue the petals onto the correct places on A.
5. Cut out B.
6. Glue B onto A.
7. Done.

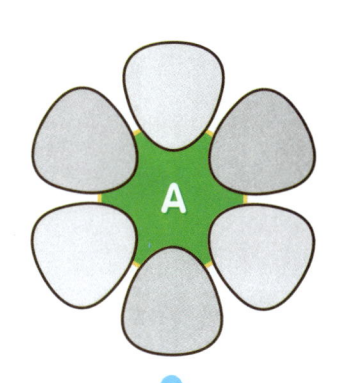

Glue B onto A.

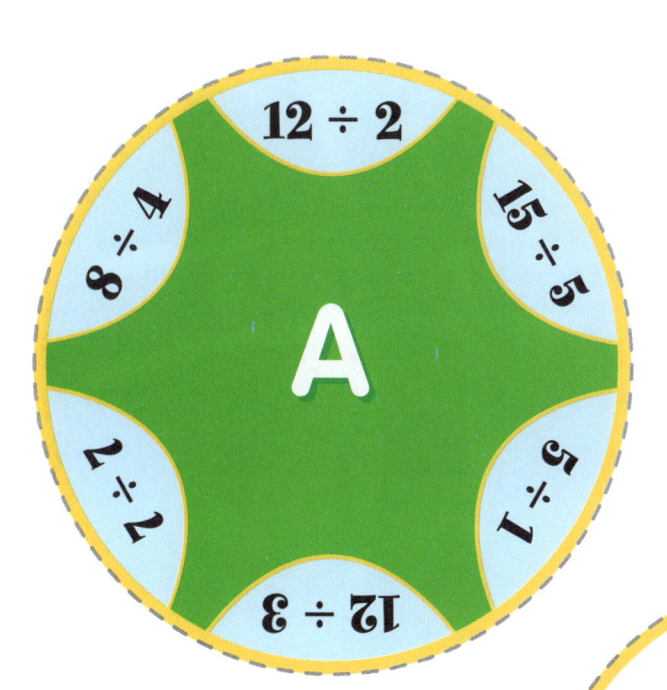

A:
- 12 ÷ 2
- 15 ÷ 5
- 5 ÷ 1
- 12 ÷ 3
- 7 ÷ 2
- 8 ÷ 4

B Glue onto A

Grade 2-3

ISBN: 978-1-897457-97-9

Hands-on

Grade 2-3

195
ISBN: 978-1-897457-97-9

ISBN: 978-1-897457-97-9

A Funny Dice

Cut along the dotted line to make a dice.

2 or more players

Each player takes turns to throw the dice. Name something that is in the category of what the dice shows within five seconds to score one point. Spell the word correctly within another five seconds to score a bonus point.

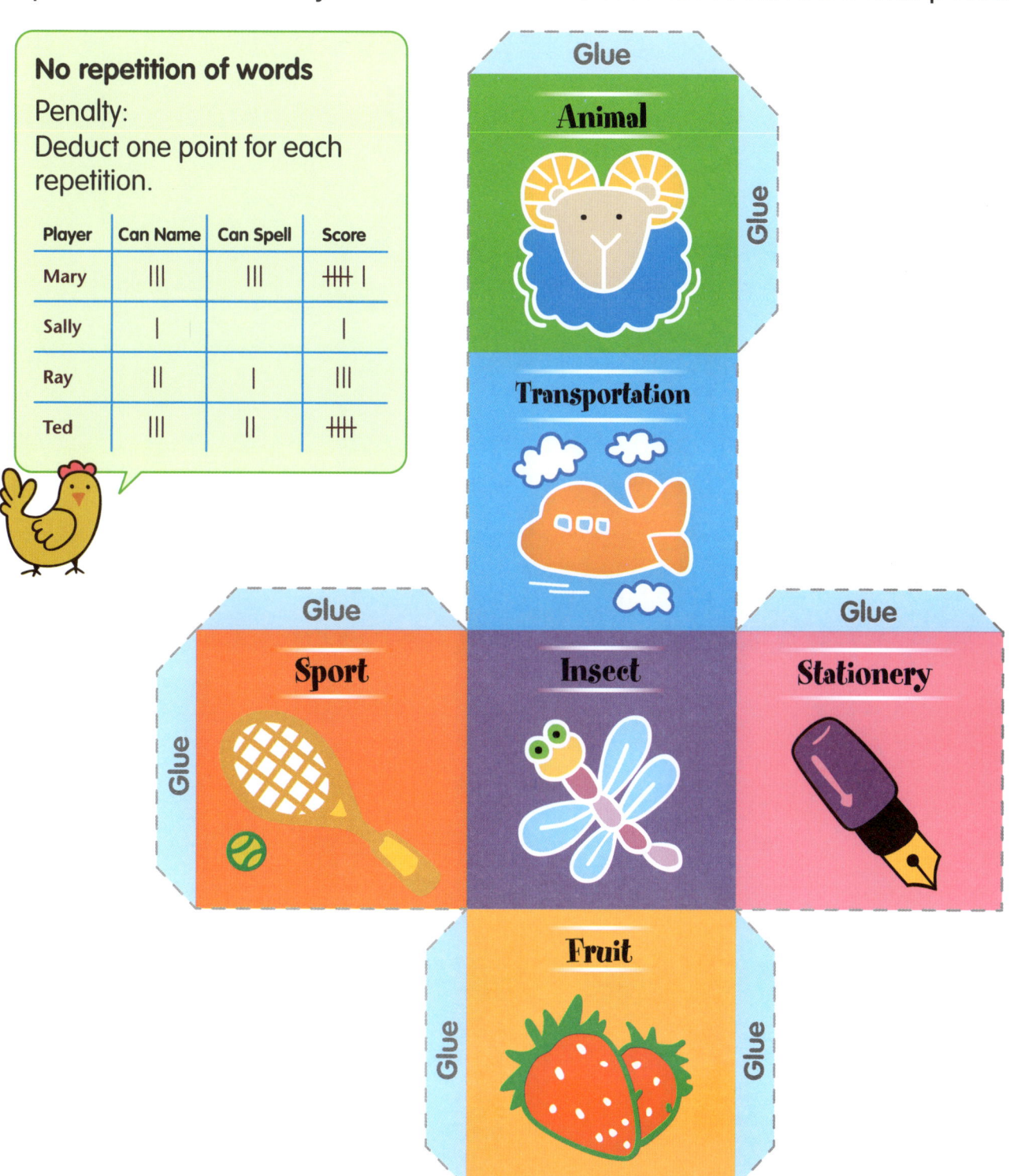

No repetition of words

Penalty:
Deduct one point for each repetition.

Player	Can Name	Can Spell	Score
Mary	|||	|||	|||||	
Sally					
Ray	||			|||
Ted	|||	||	|||||

Dice faces: Animal, Transportation, Sport, Insect, Stationery, Fruit

197

Grade 2-3

ISBN: 978-1-897457-97-9

ISBN: 978-1-897457-97-9

A Spelling Game

Cut out the pieces on this page and on page 201.

2 or more players

Place all the pieces face down in a stack. Each player takes turns to draw a piece from the top. Spell the word for the thing in the picture within 10 seconds. The number in the corner of each picture shows the point(s) the player can get for the correct spelling. When all the pieces are drawn, each player adds up the total to see who gets the highest score.

Answers:

skirt ; flute ; acorn ; mango ; beaver ; celery ; dragon ; hammer ; puppet ; rocket ; cactus ; spider ; scooter ; penguin ; feather ; lobster ; dolphin ; giraffe ; scissors ; hedgehog ; kangaroo ; mushroom ; calendar ; lollipop ; snowflake ; scorpion ; ambulance ; fireworks ; thermometer ; nutcracker ; wheelbarrow ; helicopter

ISBN: 978-1-897457-97-9

Hands-on

You can make a chart to record your scores.

Player \ Round	1st	2nd	3rd
Mary	2		
Sally	4		
Ray	1		

Grade 2-3

ISBN: 978-1-897457-97-9

ISBN: 978-1-897457-97-9

Tangram Fun

Cut out the tangram. You can use the pieces to form the things shown on this page. Then you can use the pieces to make your own pictures.

Grade 2-3

ISBN: 978-1-897457-97-9

A Precious Treasure Chest

Trace the dotted lines of the treasure chest. Cut out the lid and the body of the chest. Then glue the tabs together.

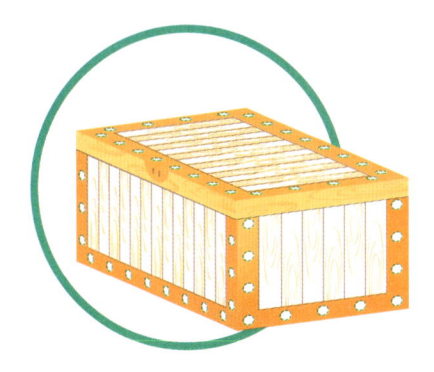

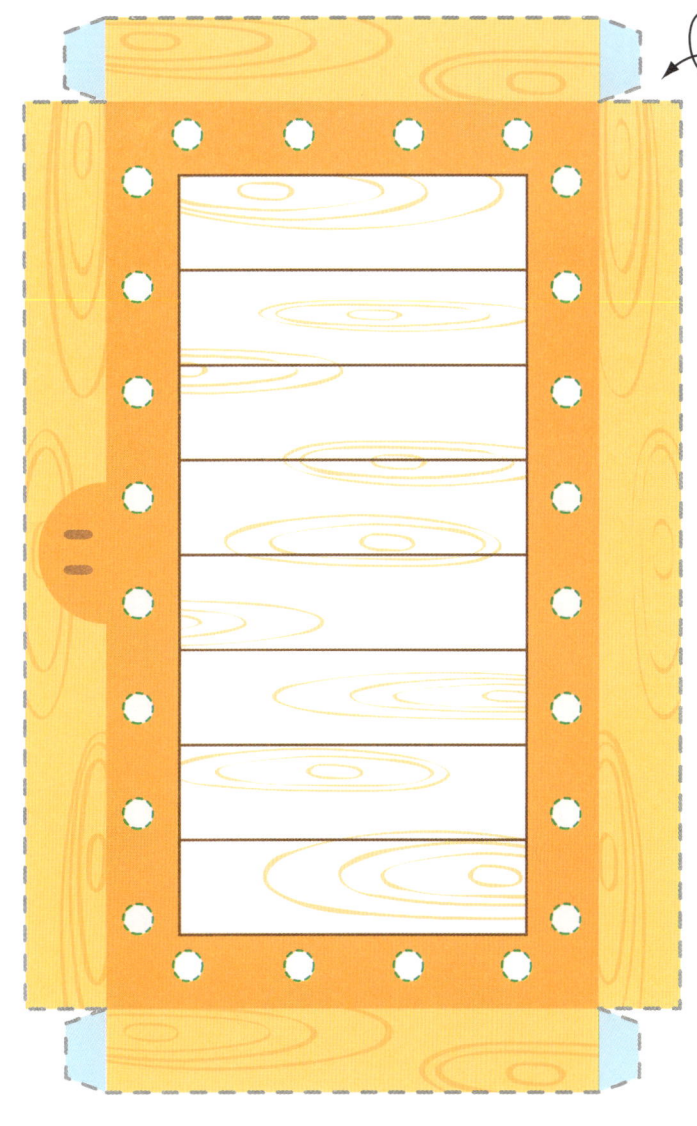

lid

You can cut out these treasures and put them in the chest.

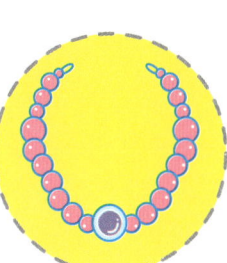

205

Grade 2-3

ISBN: 978-1-897457-97-9

ISBN: 978-1-897457-97-9

Hands-on

body

Glue Glue Glue Glue

207

Grade 2-3

ISBN: 978-1-897457-97-9

ISBN: 978-1-897457-97-9